VOCABULARY
through **Morphemes**

Second Edition

Suffixes, Prefixes, and Roots for Intermediate and Secondary Grades

Susan M. Ebbers

Cambium
LEARNING® | Sopris
Group

ISBN 13: 978-1-60697-520-6
ISBN 10: 1-60697-520-X

279793/12-14

Printed in the United States of America

Published and distributed by

4093 Specialty Place • Longmont, Colorado 80504 • (303) 651-2829
www.soprislearning.com

Contents

Student Book Answer Key Contents

Susan Ebbers is a doctoral candidate specializing in morphological awareness and vocabulary development, measurement design and interpretation, and interest theory. In the past, she taught reading to first and second grade students and intervention reading to middle school students. She has served as a preschool director and K–8 principal, working in public and private school systems. She has been named "outstanding secondary teacher" by the Tracy Unified School District and recognized by San Joaquin County, California, as an A+ literacy leader, having served as a district middle school and high school strategic literacy coach. Susan consults for several states and school districts and provides professional seminars on various topics. Samples of her publications and presentations are available online at her web site: www. readingway.com. She also publishes *Vocabulogic*, a blog dedicated to teaching morphology and vocabulary.

ACKNOWLEDGMENTS

There would not be a second edition of *Vocabulary Through Morphemes* if there had not been so much enthusiasm for the first edition. I am grateful for this—it has been rewarding to see teachers and students across the country experience a "root awakening" as they become word curious, word savvy, and word aware. This new consumable edition responds to feedback from teachers who have used *Vocabulary Through Morphemes* in the past six years. We have all attempted to learn how best to prompt morphological awareness so that vocabulary and comprehension improve. I am thankful to have seen this transmutation of critical content from technical research to professional practice. Teachers, thank you! Please keep the feedback coming.

The first edition would not have been developed without the support of the Tracy Unified School District, especially the principal, Dr. Denise Laven. Even closer to the project, I appreciate the eager attitude demonstrated by my middle school students, for whom I wrote these materials, and who served as barometers of program effect. I acknowledge several teachers who piloted the materials as they were developed, providing immediate feedback for the purpose of improving the work, including Karen Romney, Lisetta Wallace, and Mary Johnson. I extend my thanks to experts and advisers who provided consultation, including Louisa Moats, Louise Malandra, and Linda Farrell. I am indebted to the fine folks at Sopris Learning, especially to my perspicacious editor, Linda Bevard; to designer Sherri Rowe, who created outstanding page layouts; and to my formidable project manager, Michelle LaBorde. Finally, I offer my warmest regards to Chris, for technical support and encouragement and for putting up with far too many sketchy meals.

CAVEAT

This book is by no means an authoritative reference book. Numerous sources were consulted when creating it. At times, linguistic information differed slightly. At other times, the information was deemed too esoteric for the goals of this book. In that case, the interpretation most practical for improving vocabulary was chosen. If I have erred at times in synthesizing a variety of linguistic information into a program applicable to general education, the mistake is my own.

English is thought to be the most complex of all the European languages, in part because of its mongrel mixture of Greek, Latin, French (which is based in Latin), and Germanic roots (Frost, 2005; Seymour, 2005). In addition, English is generally thought to contain significantly more words and expressions than any other language (Crystal, 1995). This is useful if you are a writer in search of the perfect phrase, but for striving readers and language learners, it can be a nightmare. These two factors—the mixed complexity of English spellings and the size and scope of the lexicon—comprise a challenge for students and teachers alike. *Vocabulary Through Morphemes: Suffixes, Prefixes, and Roots for Intermediate and Secondary Grades* was written to address that challenge.

Vocabulary Through Morphemes was designed to promote structural analysis, referred to hereafter as morphological awareness (MA). *Morphology* refers to the structure of words through the smallest elements of meaning—*morphemes*—prefixes, roots, base words, and suffixes. Morphological awareness may be viewed as the ability and aptitude to infer word meaning and/or grammatical function through morphemes. English derivations such as *boyishly* or *solidarity* are morphosyntactic in nature, conveying syntax through the suffix (e.g., most words that end with -*ly* are adverbs, and most words that end with -*ity* are abstract nouns, as in *purity, salinity, security*). Furthermore, English words are morphophonemic—the spelling of a word conveys information relating to morphemic meaning and phonological sound, or pronunciation. Because the brain constantly seeks patterns and rule-governed assemblies (Pinker, 1999) children do indeed develop MA, but it is often buried in the recesses of the mind. However, this type of knowledge can become metacognitive through instruction (Nagy, 2007). In fact, MA is thought to be a subset of metacognition (McBride-Chang, Wagner, Muse, et al., 2005; Nagy, 2007). Until about 1990, MA had been somewhat overlooked in research and particularly in practice, but recent studies have shown it to be strongly related to literacy, including reading, spelling, vocabulary, comprehension, and even grammar (Carlisle, 2003; Nagy, 2007). In describing how the brain processes printed language, Wolf (2007) stated, "Morphological knowledge is a wonderful dimension of the child's uncovering of 'what's in a word,' and one of the least exploited aids to fluent comprehension."

I developed these materials as I was teaching, to help my own middle school intervention literacy class develop greater confidence and competence when faced with complex words composed of multiple affixes or combining forms. The morphemic meanings in the book are not to be memorized by rote so much as applied. Students practice inferring meaning when they encounter unknown words by combining context clues with morpheme clues, applying the outside-in strategy. With *Vocabulary Through Morphemes*, teachers convey effective independent reading habits and encourage learners to transfer their morphology skills to all aspects of reading and writing. As you teach, maintain a positive, lighthearted tone—the goal is not that the students become linguists, but that they become interested in words and aware of patterns (see Ebbers and Denton, 2008).

Using *Vocabulary Through Morphemes*, students learn to analyze the structure of words and to use context clues to find meaning. In addition, they practice sorting related words by connotation or shades of meaning, creating networks (such as *unbending, firm, unchanging, resolute, unequivocal,* and *rigid*). A major goal of the book is to help students see the patterns in morphological families of words that share a common root (*structure, construct, deconstruct, reconstruction, instructor,* etc.). In addition, the book includes analogies to help thinkers develop logic using word relationships.

Vocabulary Through Morphemes enables students both to deepen their present word knowledge and to better understand unknown words encountered in the future. Vocabulary growth should be seen in terms of breadth of knowledge (how many words do you know?) and depth of knowledge (how well do you know the words that you do know?), as described by Bowers and Kirby (2009) and Baumann, Edwards, Font et al. (2002). Through morphemic analysis in context, known words can become known at a deeper level: Students will know not only what the word means, but why it means what it means, or how it got its name, as well as how the context can—and often does—morph the meaning, slanting or reshaping it a bit.

This book teaches the more common prefixes, suffixes, and roots. The specific Greek, Latin/French, and Anglo-Saxon/Germanic morphemes and their meanings and origins were obtained from several sources (e.g., American Heritage Dictionary, 2000; Cornog, 1998; Ehrlich, 1968; Hendricks, 1992; Henry, 2003; Moats, 2000; Nurnberg and Rosenblum, 1989; Oxford English Dictionary, 2002; Stahl, 1999). These morphemes are worthy of instructional time because readers will encounter them repeatedly in varied domains, and because understanding derivational morphology is key to grasping academic content vocabulary, especially in science and social studies (Butler, Bailey, Stevens, et al., 2004). Furthermore, many of the vocabulary selections are taken from the *Academic Word List* (Coxhead, 2000) and thus increase comprehension of the formal language used in lectures, texts, and formalized tests.

CURRICULUM GOALS

One of the goals of *Vocabulary Through Morphemes* is to foster interest in and engagement with words. Another is to learn the meanings of key *morphemes* (prefixes, roots, suffixes) and to promote fluent reading of morphologically complex words. A third goal is to increase vocabulary knowledge. However, the ultimate goal is for students to confidently infer unknown word meanings during independent reading in any subject area. Students can be taught to make this inference by combining information gleaned from the outside clues (the context that surrounds the word) and the inside clues (the morphemes inside the word). This is called the outside-in strategy (Ebbers and Denton, 2008). Specific objectives include the following:

- Fluently read morphologically complex words, including academic words

- Analyze compound words, describing how they convey meaning

- State the meaning and grammatical function of the more common affixes and roots

- Analyze morphologically complex derivations that involve affixation to a root

- Use word and sentence clues to determine the meaning of unknown words

- Apply a independent word-learning strategy to connected text (outside-in strategy)

- Describe the relationships expressed in analogies

- Describe the denotations and connotations of a set of synonyms

- Create networks of antonyms, synonyms, and morphologically related words

- Develop greater competence with morphologically complex academic words

- Chronicle main events in the history of the English language

- Trace the historical origins of various English words (e.g., Latin/French, German, Greek)

Vocabulary Through Morphemes (VTM) reflects the academic content standards for English/language arts spanning grades 4–12 in many states, including California, Texas, and Florida. VTM targets specific learning expectations pertaining to structural analysis, affixes, roots, analogies, and word relationships. Grade-level expectations pertaining to word origins (including etymologies and the history of the English language), connotations and shades of meaning, and use of context clues are also addressed in this program. VTM embodies academic language and incorporates the scholarly meanings found in the *Academic Word List* (Coxhead, 2000), promoting comprehension of the formal language used in lectures, texts, and assessments. Most of the Greek roots taught in VTM are the basis for scientific terms (*biomass, thermonuclear, hydroscopic*). Although VTM is not strictly a phonics program, students learn to decode longer words in morphemic chunks. Spelling improves, because word formation rules are peppered throughout, such as "drop the final *-e* before adding a suffix that begins with a vowel" including *-y*, *-ive*, *-ity*, *-ate*, and so on. Students practice "morphological math" when they combine multiple affixes with a root, making all the necessary spelling adjustments as they do so and successfully reading long, morphologically complex words. Also, grammar improves as students learn that the derivational suffix determines the part of speech. For example, words ending with the suffix *-ful* tend to be adjectives, as with *joyful* and *plentiful*, but words ending with the suffix *-ion* tend to be nouns, as when we change the verb *educate* to the noun *education*, or we change the verb *divide* to the noun *division*.

SEQUENCE, PACING, AND TIMING

It is most effective to teach the four units—introduction, suffixes, prefixes, and roots—in the sequence provided. This is a systematic approach to learning the most common morphemes in the English language, yet it is also a spiraling curriculum, because previously learned morphemes are folded in to new lessons even as the content becomes more complex and cognitively challenging.

Introductory unit: First, set the stage—teach the brief introductory unit on the history of the English language. Then teach suffixes, prefixes, and finally roots.

Suffix unit: Students often know what a word means, basically, but they misuse it in context, perhaps using an adjective as a noun. Derivational suffixes drive syntax, helping us understand the grammatical function of a word. English derivations are *morphosyntactic*—syntax is encoded into the suffixes. For example, most words ending with the derivational suffix *-ic* are adjectives, as in *heroic, fantastic*, and *exotic*, and most words ending with the derivational suffix *-ate* are verbs, as in *educate, exaggerate*, and *hyperventilate*. Why does this matter? It is not uncommon for students to learn the basic meaning of a word—to get the gist—but to misuse it when speaking or writing. This happens because the student does not have a good grasp of derivational morphology—the student has not learned how a derivational suffix directs the part of speech. Changes in syntax occur when the suffix changes. Thus, *create* is a verb, as are many words that end with the suffix *-ate*, but *creative* is an adjective, as are many words that end with the suffix *-ive*, and *creativity* and *action* are abstract nouns, as are most words that end with the suffixes *-ity* and *-ion*. For learners to grasp abstract academic word meanings and become adept at using words correctly when speaking and writing, they must get a sense of the suffix and they must tune their ears to hear "the ring" of sound syntax. Note that this is not about memorizing the meanings of the suffixes—the meanings of most suffixes are cumbersome and opaque—rather, the goal is to improve grammar. If students understand syntax fairly well, yet need to broaden and deepen their vocabulary, move quickly to prefixes.

Prefixes influence word meaning. In many words, the meaning is clearly mapped into the prefix, as in *interior, exterior, posterior, anterior*, and *ulterior*. In many cases, prefixes change the flavor, or connotation, of the word. For example, <u>de</u>*port* is more negative than <u>sup</u>*port*, and <u>super</u>*molecule* is more impressive than *molecule*. Furthermore, the prefix is easy to find, because it is always at the beginning of the word—although it becomes tricky when the word has multiple prefixes, as in *insubstantial*. As students learn the prefixes, they will continue to encounter the suffixes they learned in the first section. This provides an opportunity to review suffixes and check for understanding over time. Distributed practice is a key component of this program.

Roots. Finally, students master the most common roots. Greek and Latin roots are ubiquitous to academic textbooks beginning in intermediate grades. Greek roots are essential to words used in the sciences. Most academic words contain a Greek or Latin root, so learning these morphemes should promote academic vocabulary. Previously taught suffixes and prefixes are integrated into the roots section to ensure a more complete understanding of the word. This allows the student to revisit and rehearse previously learned prefixes and suffixes.

Options: Depending on the needs of the students and the time allocated for instruction, these lessons could be truncated and combined. It is not always necessary for every student in every setting to fully explore every table on every instructional page and to complete every practice page. In some settings—for example, after-school and summer school programs—teachers have successfully truncated and combined sections, focusing on the most essential morphological skills, including suffixes and prefixes. For at-risk readers, the Latin and Greek roots are an advanced concept, but understanding the affixes is more immediately essential to literacy.

Pacing and timing: There are 90 lessons, plus several assessments. Plan for about 10–20 minutes a day, depending on the students' needs. With each instructional page, teach the new morpheme, reading aloud with the class, circling roots, discussing meaning. The next day, or for homework, students complete the practice page as modeled by the teacher. The entire program takes one full school year, if the instructional page is completed on one day and the practice page is completed on the next day. If the practice page is completed the same day as the instructional page, the program takes one full semester. Do not teach toward mastery and memorization of each vocabulary word. Rather, provide an understanding of the morphological concept and model the outside-in strategy for integrating context clues and morpheme clues to predict meaning. Then move on to the next lesson. The curriculum is recursive; previously taught concepts will be addressed again as review. On occasion, use flash cards and games (see Optional Games and Activities section, page 20) to review previously learned affixes and roots. Also, apply morphemic analysis to context frequently when reading any text. For summer school, spend about 20–30 minutes a day and combine two affixes or roots in one lesson. If time is very tight, use summer school to teach prefixes and perhaps a few roots.

A typical **instructional page** takes 10-20 minutes, depending on the group. Use this page to teach the linguistic principles with explicit and deductive methods. Prompt instructional conversations (whole group and partner). The goal of the instructional page is to learn the new morpheme, not to memorize a page of words. For suffixes, the primary goal is to develop syntactic awareness (e.g., words ending with **–ic** are adjectives).

Read the content aloud with the class at least once. If reading is not fluent, use active reading methods, including choral reading in groups and partner reading.

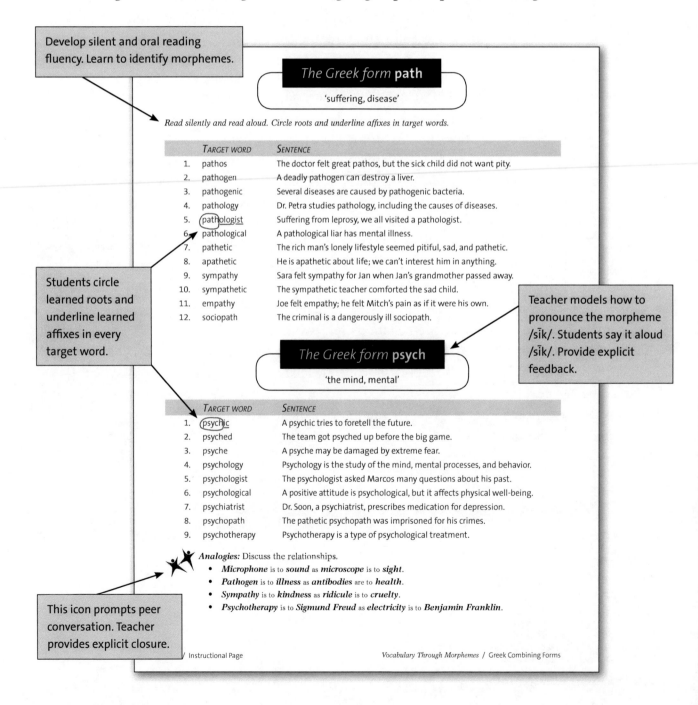

Develop silent and oral reading fluency. Learn to identify morphemes.

The Greek form **path**

'suffering, disease'

Read silently and read aloud. Circle roots and underline affixes in target words.

	TARGET WORD	SENTENCE
1.	pathos	The doctor felt great pathos, but the sick child did not want pity.
2.	pathogen	A deadly pathogen can destroy a liver.
3.	pathogenic	Several diseases are caused by pathogenic bacteria.
4.	pathology	Dr. Petra studies pathology, including the causes of diseases.
5.	pathologist	Suffering from leprosy, we all visited a pathologist.
6.	pathological	A pathological liar has mental illness.
7.	pathetic	The rich man's lonely lifestyle seemed pitiful, sad, and pathetic.
8.	apathetic	He is apathetic about life; we can't interest him in anything.
9.	sympathy	Sara felt sympathy for Jan when Jan's grandmother passed away.
10.	sympathetic	The sympathetic teacher comforted the sad child.
11.	empathy	Joe felt empathy; he felt Mitch's pain as if it were his own.
12.	sociopath	The criminal is a dangerously ill sociopath.

Students circle learned roots and underline learned affixes in every target word.

The Greek form **psych**

'the mind, mental'

Teacher models how to pronounce the morpheme /sīk/. Students say it aloud /sīk/. Provide explicit feedback.

	TARGET WORD	SENTENCE
1.	psychic	A psychic tries to foretell the future.
2.	psyched	The team got psyched up before the big game.
3.	psyche	A psyche may be damaged by extreme fear.
4.	psychology	Psychology is the study of the mind, mental processes, and behavior.
5.	psychologist	The psychologist asked Marcos many questions about his past.
6.	psychological	A positive attitude is psychological, but it affects physical well-being.
7.	psychiatrist	Dr. Soon, a psychiatrist, prescribes medication for depression.
8.	psychopath	The pathetic psychopath was imprisoned for his crimes.
9.	psychotherapy	Psychotherapy is a type of psychological treatment.

Analogies: Discuss the relationships.
- *Microphone* is to *sound* as *microscope* is to *sight*.
- *Pathogen* is to *illness* as *antibodies* are to *health*.
- *Sympathy* is to *kindness* as *ridicule* is to *cruelty*.
- *Psychotherapy* is to *Sigmund Freud* as *electricity* is to *Benjamin Franklin*.

This icon prompts peer conversation. Teacher provides explicit closure.

Instructional Page

Vocabulary Through Morphemes / Greek Combining Forms

A typical **practice page** takes 10-20 minutes, depending on the student. Ensure that students understand how to complete each type of task. Clarify the directions and model at least one example. In some cases, allow students to work with a partner. Provide explicit and timely feedback. Use these pages as a formative measure, an assessment for learning. Adjust the pace, complexity, and intensity of subsequent lessons based on this data.

Part A: *Pronouncing Greek words. When an English word flows from Greek, the final* **e** *is often pronounced, as in* **psychē**. *This is not a rule; it is a tendency.*

Read the words. Circle the words that end with a long ē sound, and mark the **e** with a line. If the word ends with a silent **e**, draw a slash through the final **e**. First, study the examples.

capé   (psychē)   apostrophe   acne

Aphrodite   catastrophe   congregate   Penelope

sesame   hyperbole   propose   epitome

Part B: *Morphotextual Mastery: Read the story. With a partner, define the bold-type words. Examine context and morphemes for clues. Then, read the story aloud.*

Greek Mythology—Aphrodite, Psyche, and Eros

The ancient Greeks created stories about gods and mortals to explain human **psychology**. In Greek mythology, Aphrodite was the goddess of love. She was exceedingly beautiful and she knew it. Aphrodite was vain and prideful—**pathetically** absorbed in her own reflection.

One day, a lovely babe named Psyche was born. Psyche was the daughter of a mortal king. As the years passed, Psyche developed into an astoundingly beautiful princess. Aphrodite became increasingly jealous of Psyche's beauty. In her **pathological** jealousy, she decided to punish the innocent princess.

Aphrodite's son, Eros, was the god of love. When he shot his invisible arrows at humans, they instantly fell in love with the first person they saw. Aphrodite told her son to make Psyche fall for an old man with rotting teeth. Eros argued with his **psychotic** mother, urging her to see a **psychotherapist**, but she would not. Finally, he agreed to do as she asked.

Standing invisible, an arrow in his hand, Eros watched Psyche. He felt **compassion** because he knew she would be miserable with the old man. Sadly he rubbed his chin, accidentally scratching himself with his own arrow. In that instant, Eros fell **passionately** and wholeheartedly in love with Psyche.

What does Aphrodite do? How does Eros fight for Psyche? Find out for yourself. Different variations of this myth are stored on the World Wide Web.

BONUS ACTIVITY   Multisensory, see page 227

Vocabulary Through Morphemes / Greek Combining Forms   Practice Page and Morphotextual Mastery / 189

Morphotextual Mastery: Students read the passage independently and discuss it with a peer. Finally, they read it aloud with a peer to promote fluent reading. This task measures the likelihood that the student will apply morphemic analysis to context.

Bonus Activity: This page is located at the end of the unit. This activity may be done any time after the student has learned the roots **psych** and **path**. Bonus pages provide for distributed, collaborative, multisensory practice.

The Objectives and Overarching Goals of Instruction

The primary reason for using *Vocabulary Through Morphemes* is not to memorize vocabulary words, even though the student's mental lexicon will expand. The ultimate goal of this curriculum is to teach students to be independent word learners through the strategic application of morphemic analysis to context. This ability—to infer word meaning by digging into external context clues and internal morpheme clues—will enable students to more confidently and capably approach academic texts, because academic texts contain a great many morphologically complex words (Baumann, Edwards, Font et al., 2002; Baumann, Edwards, Boland, et al., 2003; Edwards, Font, Baumann et al., 2004; Baumann, Ware, and Edwards, 2007; Butler et al., 2004; Nagy and Anderson, 1984).

How to Use the Instructional Pages

Use the instructional pages in *Vocabulary Through Morphemes* as a vehicle for explicit instruction and active learning. Encourage oral language, peer discussion, and silent reflection. Teach pronunciation and/or articulation of morphemes and complex words. Read aloud and read silently. Teach students to annotate each page by circling roots or base words, underlining affixes, highlighting interesting words, writing a question mark beside unknown words, and so on. Maintain a brisk pace, completing each instructional page in about 15 minutes, depending on the needs of the group.

Page title: Read the title of the page together. Be sure students can identify the language origin, the morpheme (affix or root), and the meaning. Example:

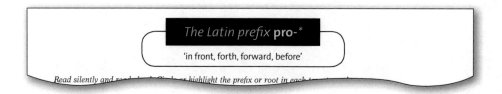

The Latin prefix **pro-***

'in front, forth, forward, before'

Read silently and ... Circle or highlight the prefix or root in each ...

- *Language origin:* Latin (remind students that Latin was used by the Romans 2000 years ago; it's no longer a spoken language, but is still used in legal documents and during religious ceremonies, and so on, and it's heard in some common expressions like "pros and cons" or "status quo")
- *Morpheme:* the prefix *pro-* (have students say and spell the morpheme)
- *Meaning: pro-* denotes 'in front, forth, forward, before' (students say the meaning)

Numbered rows of text: Give the class a minute or two to silently read the first section of numbered rows. Discuss the linguistic pattern(s). Then, have students read the text aloud, reading across each row. Use an echo-reading format in which the teacher reads a bit and students echo, or divide the class into speaking groups and have one group read each column. This is important; do not skip this step. The numbered sentences must be read aloud so students have the opportunity to say and hear the "resounding ring" of English syntax and usage.

In each row, make the relationship between columns explicit. For example, say, "See how the verb *calculate* in this column became the noun *calculation* in this column." Say, "See how the final vowel is replaced by the first vowel in the suffix. This column displays the word *create*, a word that ends in the vowel **e**. The next column displays *creative*—the final **e** is dropped when we add the suffix **-ive**."

Speaking aloud and annotating text: For each row on the instructional pages, students read silently and then they read aloud. Assign different groups of students to read the different columns in the table, reading across each row. Alternatively, read aloud in partners, one column per partner, as illustrated below. In the target words, teach students how to circle or highlight morphemes they have learned.

Encourage interest in complex words with multiple morphemes. Playfully pronounce them, treating them like tongue twisters, perhaps. Help students learn to put the accent on the correct syllable.

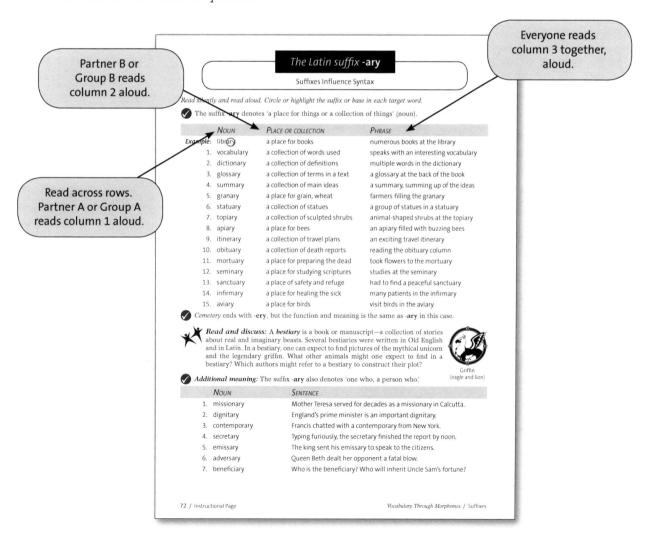

Instant Discussions—Talking Topics: Instructional pages display the to prompt brief discussions. Topics vary. As students converse with each other, the teacher walks about listening. After a few minutes, the teacher opens the discussion to the whole group, providing explicit feedback. Several different examples are shown here, with teaching tips for each type:

From Student Book page 192.

Etymology: *The Study of Word Origins*

 One of the strengths of the English language is its willingness to adopt words from foreign fields. Adopted words are called loanwords. India lent us the word *shampoo;* from the Spanish we got *amigo,* from China *ketchup,* from Arabia *sofa,* from Denmark *cookie* (originally meaning 'little cake'), and from West Africa *zombie*. From Irish/Gaelic flowed *whiskey, slogan,* and *truant. Potato* is from Haiti. Do you know any other loanwords?

TEACHING TIP: As a way to kindle interest and engagement with words, use word histories (etymologies) to illustrate that English words flow from a variety of different languages and that word meanings are prone to change over time. Consider pinning word cards on a map of the world and/or have students write words on the map on page 5 in their book.

From Student Book page 116.

 Discuss the denotations and connotations:
- How are *unfed* and *underfed* different in meaning? How are they the same?
- How are *unpaid* and *underpaid* different in meaning? How are they the same?
- Compare *uneducated* and *undereducated*. Contrast them, too.

TEACHING TIP: Use this type of talking point to illustrate that morphemes make a big difference to meaning. For example, if a person is *unfed*, that person has had no food, but if a person is *underfed*, that person has had some food, but not enough. Remind students to be precise with vocabulary when speaking and writing.

Synonyms: *Discuss the meaning, nuance, or connotations.*

childlike	childish	child
innocent, young, naïve, trusting, open, simple-minded	selfish, immature, spoiled, bratty, infantile, self-centered	baby, infant, toddler, youngster, offspring, son, daughter, kid, youth

TEACHING TIP: Use this type of talking point (1) to show how suffixes change words, from *child*, to *childlike*, to *childish*; (2) to illustrate the importance of word choice and help students become more discerning when listening or reading and more particular when speaking and writing; and (3) to make students aware of nuance, connotations, and shades of meanings. Connotations are the feelings that a word triggers, whether positive, neutral or negative. Ask partners to rank the synonymous words as positive, negative, or neutral. There is no correct answer, and responses will vary, because connotations are unique to each person based on his or her experiences with that word (authentic experiences or secondhand experiences gained through books and movies). Nevertheless, there will be some agreement for some words. For example, the words *innocent*, *open*, and *trusting* are fairly positive; *young* is neutral; but *naïve* and *simple-minded* may trigger uncomfortable feelings and negative responses—these words might be used pejoratively to insult, offend, or label people. Remind students to be aware of connotations and to be thoughtful and considerate with vocabulary when speaking and writing.

Discuss the connotations of the boldface words.

If Roman soldiers were disobedient, their **centurion** (who commanded 100 men) would decimate the troop as punishment, killing (**decimating**) every tenth soldier as they stood in a line. **Mutiny** (disobedience) resulted in **capital punishment**. The word **decimation** has fearful connotations. When should it be used?

TEACHING TIP: Use this type of talking point to teach word origins, the numeric prefix *deci-* ('ten'), and the difference between denotations (the definition of a word) and connotations (the feelings, images, and associations a word triggers). Remind students to be aware of connotations and to be thoughtful and considerate with vocabulary when speaking and writing.

From Student Book page 192.

Morphotextual Mastery. *Read. Discuss the meaning of the boldface words.*

In Greek mythology, Cronos was time itself, for he was the son of the very first god. However, time taught Cronos nothing; he was wickedly ambitious. **Eventually**, the **psycho** killed his own father. In death, his father prophesied, "In the **chronicles** of time it will come to pass that your own children will rise up and **dethrone** you, just as you have dethroned me, for crime **begets** crime!" . . . [The passage continues.]

TEACHING TIP: Brief passages allow students to apply newly learned morphemes in context (in this case, the prefixes *de-* and *be-* and the roots *psych* and *chron*). The goal is to develop an independent word learning strategy: To infer the meaning of unknown words, we look outside the word at the context clues and inside the word at the morphemes. We merge the clues and use them to validate our hypothesis. This is called the outside-in strategy. Teachers should use explicit modeling, including a think-aloud method, to teach students how to strategically glean word information from context and morphemes. With a think-aloud process, circle context clues and highlight morphemes that help a reader infer word meaning. For more details on this strategy, see student page 13.

From Student Book pages 20, 38.

Analogies: *Discuss how the words are related.*

- ***Chilly*** is to ***sweater*** as ***wintry*** is to ***overcoat***.
- ***Scrooge*** is to ***tightfistedness*** as ***Snow White*** is to ***kindheartedness***.
- ***Forgiveness*** is to ***peace*** as ***vengeance*** is to ***war***.

TEACHING TIP: Use this type of talking point to help students think analytically and to focus on grammatical word class. An analogy displays a relationship between ideas, but the relationship is not transparent or immediately obvious. The relationship between the first two words must be the same as the relationship between the second two words, creating a balanced equation.

In the example, the first analogy relates an adjective to a noun: *chilly* (adjective) weather calls for a *sweater* (noun) just as *wintry* (adjective) weather calls for an *overcoat* (noun). Tell students to highlight *chilly* and *wintry* in one color (a color used for adjectives). Highlight *sweater* and *overcoat* in another color (a color used for nouns). Under *chilly* write "cold," and under *wintry* write "even colder." Through discussion, lead the students to see that you wear a sweater when it is *chilly* and you wear an overcoat when it is *wintry*. By degree, *wintry* is colder than *chilly*.

(continued)

Academic Vocabulary

What is an academic word? Many of the exemplar words in VTM are academic words—words that replace primary-grade synonyms and that appear across domains of study. For example, a primary word is *job* and its academic counterpart is *profession*. Students might encounter the word *profession* in math, science, social studies, literature, and so on. Cross-curricular exposure makes the word more worth teaching, as does morphological relatedness.

Application: From any given instructional page, the teacher might select an academic word and teach it. Briefly elaborate on the meaning and use of the academic word. Have students generate statements that include the academic word.

PRACTICE PAGES (How To)

The practice page should take about 10 minutes, with some exceptions. In *Vocabulary Through Morphemes*, practice pages are not tests, but rather are part of the learning experience. After learning the new morpheme(s) on the instructional page, students complete the associated practice page. Through explicit instruction, ensure that learners understand the directions. Explain the examples, modeling and using think-aloud methods to make the cognitive processing transparent. Through modeling, teach students how and where to look back in previous pages for help. Include the process of referring back in the book for help in the "think-aloud" part of the lesson. Gradually reduce the amount of support as it becomes clear that the task is understood. Allow students to complete the rest of the page immediately, as homework, or at the beginning of class the next day. Make a dictionary available for reference.

In many (but not all) cases, let students complete the practice page, or part of the page, with a partner. Encourage conversation. This should help kindle interest and engagement with words. The discussion icon (✖) prompts students to collaborate and communicate with a peer. Students first work independently, reading and responding in silence, and then they discuss answers with a peer. This should deepen metacognitive knowledge.

Discuss the answers together, providing immediate and explicit feedback. Answers are provided in this guide for each lesson. Provide timely and explicit feedback in the form of validation, affirmation, and/or clarification. Re-teach when needed. Allow students to change their answers. In *Vocabulary Through Morphemes*, practice pages are not tests, but are rather part of the learning experience.

Bonus Practice Pages: *Multisensory Learning Activities*

Bonus multisensory pages are provided to further reinforce the taught concepts. Bonus pages are referenced at the foot of the correlating practice page in the Student Book. They are also referenced at the foot of the answer key in the Teachers' Guide and in the Table of Contents. Bonus pages may be used for distributed multisensory practice at any time after the relevant lesson has been learned.

Most of the practice pages review concepts learned in previous lessons. Several assessments are also provided. Use these tools to monitor student learning and plan future lessons. Provide immediate and explicit feedback on completion of the tests. Also, look for increasing interest in words. Students will begin to notice morphemes in their world. Notice an increasingly adept use of morphemic analysis in context during content-area reading. These are all indicators of morphological awareness.

In addition to definitional assessments in which students match morpheme to meaning, formative assessments are scattered liberally throughout the student book; in many cases, they are included on practice pages. Using these unique tools to measure "morphotextual mastery," teachers can assess each student's growing ability to apply newly learned morphemes to context. Even though these are called assessments, they are not intended to be viewed as tests. Rather, look at them as a way to predict how well the student will transfer learned concepts to content-area reading. Teachers can gauge how well students, even when working with a partner, understand and apply the outside-in strategy. Teachers (and peers) can immediately provide explicit feedback, and instruction can be adapted accordingly. The ability to infer word meaning by digging into external context clues and internal morpheme clues is the ultimate goal of the entire curriculum. After students complete the task, provide immediate feedback. Use the morphotextual mastery passages as opportunities to model strategic use of morphemic analysis in context.

An excerpt from the last assessment in the student book is shown here. This summative test taps into knowledge and application of suffixes, prefixes, and roots to words in context. First, the teacher leads the class in a brief discussion of the passage's title, to activate schemata (students will have read about the Romans on several prior pages). Students complete this final test alone. Fluency could be measured, too.

Final Assessment
Morphotextual Mastery: Suffixes, Prefixes, Roots

Discuss the title. Then read the passage silently. Highlight roots that you know. On the blank lines, write a suffix or prefix to complete the word. Finally, read the passage expressively.

The Wonders of Roman Engineering

If we begin with the legendary Romulus and Remus (~700 B.C.), the Roman civilization lasted more than a millennium. During this era, Rome changed technology forever. How? Romans were builders. They were excell _ent_ engineers, always dreaming up new ways to make their empire run more smoothly.

For example, to connect their vast territory they built a remark _able_ highway system. It was said, "All roads lead to Rome" (the capital city). A network of roads allowed the Romans to transport mail, import goods, and lead captives into captiv _ity_ . On well-kept Roman roads, a chariot _eer_ could quickly transmit messages. Some Roman roads still exist today, _in_ credible as it sounds.

When Rome needed a more plenti _ful_ supply of fresh water, engineers designed aqueducts. To _con_ struct these aqueducts, they rerouted water from higher elevations. Roman aqueducts were capacious, bearing approximate _ly_ 14 million gallons of water into Rome daily, on average. Romans built arched bridges across the waterways. A few bridges are still in exist _ence_ today. Modern engineers marvel at such impress _ive_ workmanship.

OPTIONAL GAMES AND ACTIVITIES

Suggestions for games and activities are provided to help ensure interest and engagement and as a means for distributed practice. Many of the activities take less than 10 minutes and some only take 3 minutes, making them ideal for downtime in the class. Teachers might use these activities occasionally to supplement the program.

Inventing Words

Have students invent new words using learned morphemic constituents. Allow students to refer to their book or their linguistics notebook, or to the Master List of Morphemes provided in this teacher's guide on page 27. Then have students work with partners to try to infer what each other's word probably means. If partner A cannot infer the word meaning, partner B could gradually give more explicit clues, providing context for the newly minted word.

Noting Newly Coined Words

Have students seek out newly coined words when they watch television, including commercials, and when they browse the Internet, listen to songs, and read newspapers, magazines, and books. For example, two relatively new terms are *blogosphere* and *Beneful* (a brand of dog food). Encourage students to share the new word or phrase with the class and to discuss how it was formed and whether it effectively conveys the desired meaning or creates the desired connotation. Finally, perhaps, have students post new words on the wall map.

Literature

Perhaps read the novel *Frindle* by Andrew Clements with the class. It is an engaging tale for fifth graders about freedom of speech, the coining of new words, etymology, the role of the dictionary, and young entrepreneurship. Other books suitable for intermediate grades are *The Unbreakable Code*, *Donovan's Word Jar*, and *Cryptomania*.

Carousels

Post about six sheets of newsprint or poster paper around the room. Write a different affix or root at the top of each one. Groups of students move from poster to poster at a prearranged signal (e.g., when the lights flash). Students carry markers and write words on the poster containing that morpheme. After 1 minute, give the signal and have the groups rotate to the next poster. Continue through all the posters. Then, read the posters together as a class and discuss any intriguing words.

Option: Write a different word—not root—on each poster. Have students add related words to the page. For example, for the *act* poster, they might add the related derivations *actor, actress, active, actively, activation, react, reacted, reactor*, and so on.

Jeopardy®

A Jeopardy grid is provided among the Teacher Extras on the CD that accompanies this book. Headings could include: *-ive* or *-age* suffix; Latin roots; *anti-* or *dis-* prefix; Greek forms; 'one who _____'; 'full of _____'; and so forth. Have clues prepared to read aloud for each point value. Preselect some as double value.

Example: Under the heading '*-ive* or *-age* suffix' for 100 points, you could read this clue: 'a tendency to sense feelings' and award 100 points for the correct answer *sensitive* (not *sensage*).

Bingo

Various bingo grids are provided among the Teacher Extras on the CD that accompanies this book. Have students choose from a given list of possible affixes or roots and have them write their choices into their grid. Call out definitions that match the morpheme, from the choices bank.

Relays

Write two different affixes or roots on the board, like *tele* and *bio*. Divide the class into two teams. Within a set time (2 or 3 minutes), team members hurry to the board, one at a time, and write a word containing that affix or root. They do this relay-race style. When the timer goes off, the team that has the most correct related words wins. For example, for the suffix *-ship*, answers include *friendship*, *courtship*, and *companionship*.

Blackboard Boggle

Draw a grid 3 × 3 square on the board. Put a root or base word in the center and affixes around it. Students form two teams. The team captain acts as scribe at the board, and team members take turns forming words. One point is scored for each letter of each word. As in the real Boggle® game, you cannot jump over a square. So, you could not spell *actionable*, because the *-ion* does not touch the *-able* square. Nor could you spell *reactionary*. Possible answers in the example shown are *active, actively, action, react, reactive, reaction, reactor, activate*.

re-	-ly	-ary
-or	act	-ive
-able	-ate	-ion

Morpho-Graphic Posters

For the target word, students will make a morpho-graphic poster showing colorful, stylistic word art. In the large box, they write each morpheme in large print, using a different color or format for each one. In smaller print, they label each prefix, base, or root with its meaning. They label the final suffix with the word class (noun, adjective, verb, or adverb). On the two lines below the box, they use the word in a sentence. See example on this page.

Root Tree

Students write the root at the base of the tree. They write derivatives along the branches, clustering the words together in similar groupings. See completed root tree below and also see student page 219 (root tree for *press*). A blank root tree is provided in the Teacher Extras section on the CD that accompanies this book.

For the target word, make a morpho-graphic poster showing colorful, stylistic word art. In the large box, write each morpheme in large print, using a different color or format for each one. In smaller print, label each prefix, base, or root with its meaning. Label the final suffix with the word class (noun, adjective, verb, or adverb). On the two lines below the box, use the word in a sentence. Share your creativity with others.

Example: creatively

create + -ive + -ly

('to make') ('tendency to') (adverb)

Target word: _____

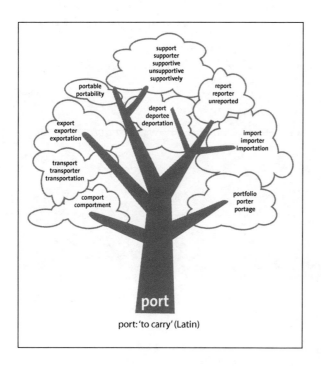

port: 'to carry' (Latin)

Academic Word List (AWL)

This document lists the most frequent words (in root families) in academic texts. These 570 high-frequency academic words are ranked into 10 sublists, where words on Sublist 1 appeared more often in the academic corpus than words on Sublist 10 (Coxhead, 2000). See *Daily Oral Vocabulary Exercises: A Program to Expand Academic Language in Grades 4–12* (Ebbers and Carroll, 2010).

affix

A prefix or a suffix, collectively called affixes. To construct a complex word, we af-*fix* (verb) an *af*-fix (noun) to a root or base.

affix type: prefix

A morpheme that is "fixed" in place before (hence *pre*) the root or base.

affix type: suffix

A morpheme that is "fixed" in place after (*suf* = *sub*) the root or base.

analogy

A similarity between two things otherwise dissimilar.

antonyms

Words that are opposite or nearly opposite in meaning.

assimilation

Assimilation occurs naturally, through speech. It happens when the final sound of the prefix is assimilated into the first sound of the base. The similar sounds flow together, making the word easier to pronounce.

cognates

Words in different languages that stem from a common root or origin and share similarities in meaning and spelling. The word pairs *prosperity/prosperidad* and *insect/insecto* are two examples of English/Spanish cognates.

etymology

The origin and historical development of a linguistic form, including a historical account of how a word or phrase changes in meaning, usage, and spelling over time.

Greek combining form

A morpheme, usually bound. Greek forms are typically more stable in meaning than Latin roots. Unlike Latin, Greek combining forms need not be used in a strict prefix–root–suffix sequence. Examples: *tele, phone, graph*. Greek combining forms are constructed much like compound words, as in *telephone* and *phonograph*. Perhaps to maintain simplicity, many schoolbooks use the term "root" to mean Greek combining form.

lexicon

A dictionary or word listing. Also, the mental lexicon comprises words, idiomatic expressions, and morphemes known by a person.

metalinguistic awareness

An acquired and heightened awareness of language; the ability to reflect on all aspects of language—pronunciation, tone, accent, spelling, meaning, syntax, awareness of rhyme, onomatopoeia, alliteration, word order, prosody and expression, phrasing, and so on (includes word consciousness and morphological awareness).

morpheme

Morpheme derives from Greek *morph*, for 'small form or shape.' A morpheme is the smallest unit of meaning in a word, including prefixes, roots or base words, and suffixes. The word *readers* has three morphemes: *read, -er*, and *-s*. The word *improbability* has four morphemes: *im-, -prob-, -able, -ity*. The compound word *foghorn* has two morphemes: *fog* and *horn*.

morpheme type: bound morpheme

A morpheme that does not stand alone as an English word. For example, the Latin root *spect* ('to see') is a bound morpheme, because in order to become an English word, it must be "bound" to a prefix and/or suffix, as in *spectacles* and *respect*.

morpheme type: free morpheme

A morpheme that stands alone as an English word, as in the base word *accept* in the derived word *acceptable*. Most free morphemes are base words, and many derive from the Germanic layer of the English language.

morphological awareness

Morphological awareness may be viewed as the ability and aptitude to infer word meaning, spelling, and/or grammatical function through the constituent morphemes. This construct includes an *interest* in words and word structure and an awareness of morphological relationships such as seen in the family *mystic, mystical, mystery, mystify, demystify*, and so on.

morphological word family

Words that share the same root or base—for example, c*ourage, discourage, encourage, courageous*, and so on.

morphology

Morphology is also called structural analysis. In English, morphology is the study of how words and meanings are constructed and conveyed by adding or subtracting prefixes, suffixes, base words, and/or roots.

network of related words

Words that are commonly associated, including synonyms, antonyms, derivations, and so on (*transportation, transport, bus, ship, travel, move, passenger,* etc.)

root

A morpheme, usually bound. A Latin root does not usually stand alone as an English word. Examples: *nat* is the Latin root in *nature, native,* and *nativity.* The Latin suffix *-ure* was added to the root to construct the English derivative *nature.*

suffix type: derivational suffixes

Suffixes that direct the syntax, word class, or part of speech. For example, adding the derivational suffix *-ive* will change *mass* from a noun to an adjective (*massive*).

suffix type: inflectional suffixes

Suffixes that do not change the part of speech of the form to which they are affixed. Inflectional suffixes change the noun from singular to plural (*box* to *boxes*) or they change the tense of the verb (*talk, talked, talking*). The comparative and superlative forms *-er* and *-est* are also inflectional suffixes. These suffixes do not change the syntax, so they are inflectional: *cold, colder,* and *coldest* are all adjectives. (However, the *-er* suffix in *teacher* is a derivational suffix, because it changes the verb *teach* to a noun, *teacher.*)

synonyms

Words that are the same or nearly the same in meaning.

word origins

The language of birth for a given word. For example, *sugar* is Persian from Sanskrit, *algebra* is Arabic, and *fiesta* is Spanish. More than 90 percent of English words originated from German (about 22 percent of English words, usually common everyday words), Latin and Latin/French/Norman (about 60 percent, often academic words), or Greek (about 12 percent, often pertaining to the sciences, mythology, and performing arts).

word origins web site

To determine a word's origin and/or etymology, type in the word in the search field at www.etymonline.com. For example, the etymology for the word *algebra* is given as:

> 1550s [the year the word is thought to have entered the English language], from M.L. [Middle Latin] from Arabic *al jebr* "reunion of broken parts," as in computation, used 9c. [ninth century] by Baghdad mathematician Abu Ja'far Muhammad ibn Musa al-Khwarizmi as the title of his famous treatise on equations ("*Kitab al-Jabr w'al-Muqabala*" "Rules of Reintegration and Reduction"), which also introduced Arabic numerals to the West. The accent shifted 17c. from second syllable to first. The word was used in Eng. 15c.-16c. to mean "bone-setting," probably from the Arabs in Spain.

word type: base word

A free morpheme. A base word can stand alone if the affixes are removed. For example, *house* is the base word in *houses*, and *child* is the base word in *children*. Many English base words are Germanic/Anglo-Saxon/Old English in origin.

word type: complex word

A complex word is composed of several morphemes, such as *consolidate, allegorical, redistribution*, and *overemphasis*.

word type: compound word

Compound words are constructed by joining two or more base words. Compounds can be joined, hyphenated, or set apart, as in *lighthouse, son-in-law*, and *polar bear*. The Germanic/Anglo-Saxon layer of the English language includes a large number of compound words.

MASTER LIST OF MORPHEMES— SUFFIXES, PREFIXES, ROOTS

Suffix	Meaning	Syntax*	Exemplars
-er	one who, that which	noun	teacher, clippers, toaster
-er	more	adjective	faster, stronger, kinder
-ly	to act in a way that is . . .	adjective	kindly, decently, firmly
-able	capable or worthy of	adjective	honorable, predictable
-ible	capable of, worthy of	adjective	terrible, responsible, visible
-hood	condition of being	noun	childhood, statehood, falsehood
-ful	full of, having	adjective	wonderful, spiteful, dreadful
-less	without	adjective	hopeless, thoughtless, fearless
-ish	somewhat like	adjective	childish, foolish, snobbish
-ness	condition or state of	noun	happiness, peacefulness, fairness
-ic	relating to	adjective	energetic, historic, volcanic
-ist	one who	noun	pianist, balloonist, specialist
-ian	one who	noun	librarian, historian, magician
-or	one who	noun	governor, editor, operator
-eer	one who	noun	mountaineer, pioneer, commandeer, profiteer, engineer, musketeer
o-logy	study of	noun	biology, ecology, mineralogy
-ship	art or skill of, condition, rank, group of	noun	leadership, citizenship, companionship, kingship
-ous	full of, having, possessing	adjective	joyous, jealous, nervous, glorious, victorious, spacious, gracious
-ive	tending to...	adjective	active, sensitive, creative
-age	result of an action	noun	marriage, acreage, pilgrimage
-ant	a condition or state	adjective	elegant, brilliant, pregnant
-ant	a thing or a being	noun	mutant, coolant, inhalant

* The syntax column indicates the most likely grammatical function of words ending with the given suffix.

Suffix	Meaning	Syntax*	Exemplars
-ent	someone who, something that	noun	student, president, nutrient
-ent	inclined to	adjective	different, fluent, persistent
-ment	state or act of	noun	payment, basement, improvement
-ary	place for, collection of	noun	glossary, granary, library
-ary	relating to, condition	adjective	secondary, military, necessary
-ary	one who	noun	secretary, dignitary, emissary
-ize	to make	verb	hypnotize, fertilize, centralize
-ise	to make	verb	advise, advertise, improvise
-ure	action or condition of	noun	moisture, mixture, pleasure
-ion	act or condition	noun	action, friction, fusion, mission
-ation	act or condition	noun	starvation, condensation
-ance	act or condition of	noun	assistance, endurance, importance
-ence	act or condition of	noun	persistence, excellence, confidence
-ity	state or quality of	noun	prosperity, equality, security
-al	relating to	adjective	magical, comical, logical
(ti)-al	relating to	adjective	spatial, initial, essential
(si)-al	relating to	adjective	official, social, artificial
-ate	to make	verb	calculate, activate, participate
-ate	state or quality of	adjective	desolate, ultimate, literate
-tude	condition of	noun	solitude, exactitude, fortitude
-ism	practice, belief	noun	feudalism, racism, monotheism

* The syntax column indicates the most likely grammatical function of words ending with the given suffix.

Prefix	Meaning(s)	Exemplars
de-	from, reduce, or opposite	defrost, dethrone, dehydration
dis-	opposite	disagree, disadvantage, dishonest
trans-	across, over, through	transfer, translate, transcontinental
dia-	across, through	diagonal, diagnostic, diameter
ex-	out, from	expel, excavate, expatriate, exhale
e-	out, from	erase, evict, emit, evaporate, evacuate
mono-	one, single	monoplane, monopoly, monorail
uni-	one, single	unicycle, unicorn, universal
bi-	two	bicycle, biped, bilateral
di-	two, or in parts	digraph, divert, diameter
tri-	three	tricycle, triangle, triune
multi-	many, much	multicolored, multimillionaire
poly-	many, much	polygon, polyhedron, polyester
pre-	before	predict, prepare, preheat
post-	after	postwar, postscript, postdate
mal-	bad, evil	malcontent, maladjusted, malnutrition
mis-	wrong, bad	mistake, misspell, misunderstand
bene-	good, well	benefit, beneficial, benediction
pro-	forward, forth, before	protector, procreate, profession
sub-	under, beneath	substitute, subtraction, subway
re-	back, again	rewind, remember, retaliate
inter-	among, between	interstate, internet, interpersonal
intra-	within	intranet, intravenous, intranasal
co-	together, with	cooperate, coworker, copilot
com-	together, with	company, commit, committee
con-	together, with	concur, concert, contingent
col-	together, with	colleague, collide, collaborate
be-	to, completely	befriend, belie, belittle, bejeweled
non-	not	nonsense, nonrefundable, nonprofit
un-	not	uncomfortable, uncertain, untrue

Prefix	Meaning(s)	Exemplars
in-	not	incapable, inedible, intolerant
im-	not	imperfect, immoral, imbalanced
il-	not	illiterate, illogical, illegal
ir-	not	irregular, irresponsible
in- (im-, il-, ir-)	in, into, on, upon (this prefix has two meanings: 'not' and 'in')	inside, insert, implant, impostor, infuriate, inflammable, incandescent
a-	not, negative	amoral, atonal, atheist
an-	not, negative	anarchist, anomaly, anathema
anti-	against, opposite	antiseptic, anticrime, antitrust, antisocial
contra-	against, opposite	contradict, contrary, contraceptive
counter-	against, opposite	counterclockwise, counterfeit, counterbalance
en-	to cause to be, to put or go into or onto	enable, enrich, engulf, enflame
em-	to cause to be, to put or go into or onto	employ, embark, embellish

Greek Root	Meaning(s)	Exemplars
astr-o	stars, heavens	astronaut, astrology, astronomer
bi-o	life	biography, biosphere, biology
ge-o	earth, rocks	geology, geographer, geothermal
therm	heat, warm	thermostat, thermal, exothermic
aut-o	self	autism, automatic, autoimmune, autograph
hom-o	same, alike	homonym, homogenize, homophone
hydr-o	water	hydrogen, hydrology, hydroelectric
micro	small	microscope, microclimate, microcosm
macro	large	macroclimate, macroevolution
phon-o	sound, speech	telephone, phonics, symphony
scope	instrument used to observe, to see	telescope, microscope, kaleidoscope
graph	written	autograph, telegraph, geographer
phot-o	light	photograph, photon, photobiotic
tele	distant, far	telescope, television, telecommunications
meter, metr	instrument used to measure	metric, thermometer, barometer, chronometer
path, pass	suffering, disease	psychopath, pathogen, sympathy, compassion
psych-o	mind, mental	psychology, psychic, psychotropic
pan	all, whole	panorama, panacea, pantomime, pandemonium
zoo	animal	zoology, zootoxin, zoogeography
chron	time	chronic, chronological, synchronized
phobia	fear, intense dislike	claustrophobia, xenophobic, arachnophobia

Latin Root	Meaning(s)	Exemplars
port	to carry	transport, export, porter, portal, reporter
form	to shape	formation, reform, conform, formulation
tract	to pull	tractor, subtract, detract, traction, retractable
rupt	to break	disrupt, interrupt, rupture, corrupt
spect, spec	to see, to watch	inspect, suspect, spectator, respect, specimen
struct, stru	to build	construct, structure, instruct, construe
dict, dic	to tell, to say	dictionary, dictate, predict, indicate
flec, flex	to bend	flexible, reflector, genuflect, inflection, reflective
cred	to believe	credit, credentials, credulous, incredible
aqua	water	aquatic, aquarium, aquamarine
pel, puls	to drive, push	propel, compel, impel, repel, impulse, pulsate
fact, fac	to make, to do	factory, facilitate, factor, faction, factotum
ject	to throw, to throw down	inject, projectile, reject, subject, conjecture
vert, vers	to turn	reverse, versatile, convert, revert, divert
mit, mis	to send	missile, missionary, admission, emit, transmit
mort	to die	mortal, mortician, mortuary
script, scrib	to write	scribble, script, scripture, prescription
junct	to join	conjunction, junction, adjunct, juncture
cide	to kill, a killer	suicide, genocide, homicide
press	to force, squeeze	press, impress, express, compress, repress
spire	to breathe	respire, respiration, respiratory, conspire, inspire, perspire, expire, spirit, spirited, spiritual
grad, gress	to step	graduate, gradual, gradations, regress, congress, digress, transgress, egress, progression
cept, capt	to take, seize, receive	capture, captivity, intercept, exception

REFERENCES

American Heritage Dictionary, 4th ed. (2000). Boston: Houghton Mifflin.

Baumann, J.F., Edwards, E.C, Font, G., Tereshinski, C.A., Kame'enui, E.J., and Olejnik, S. (2002). Teaching morphemic and contextual analysis to fifth-grade students. *Reading Research Quarterly, 37*(2), 150–176.

Baumann, J.F., Edwards, E.C., Boland, E., Olejnik, S., and Kame'enui, E.J. (2003). Vocabulary tricks: Effects of instruction in morphology and context on fifth-grade students' ability to derive and infer word meaning. *American Educational Research Journal, 40,* 447–494.

Baumann, J.F., Ware, D., and Edwards, E.C. (2007). Bumping into spicy, tasty words that catch your tongue: A formative experiment on vocabulary instruction. *The Reading Teacher, 61*(2), 108–122.

Bowers, P. and Kirby, J. (2009). Effects of morphological instruction on vocabulary acquisition. *Journal of Reading and Writing.* Retrieved online 7-2-09.

Butler, F. A., Bailey, A. L., Stevens, R., Huang, B., and Lord, C. (2004). *Academic English in fifth-grade mathematics, science, and social studies textbooks. CSE report 642.* Center for the Study of Evaluation (CSE)/National Center for Research on Evaluation, Standards, and Student Testing (CRESST). Retrieved 7-2-09 from www.csa.com.

Carlisle, J. F. (2003). Morphology matters in learning to read: A commentary. *Reading Psychology, 24*(3), 291–322.

Cornog, M. (1998). *Merriam-Webster's Vocabulary Builder.* Springfield, MA: Merriam-Webster, Inc.

Coxhead, Averil. (2000). A new academic word list. *TESOL Quarterly, 34,* 213–238. http://language.massey.ac.nz/staff/awl/index.shtml.

Crystal, D. (1995). *The Cambridge Encyclopedia of the English Language.* Cambridge, UK: Press Syndicate of University of Cambridge.

Ebbers, S.M., and Carroll, J. (2010). *Daily Oral Vocabulary Exercises: A Program to Expand Academic Language in Grades 4-12.* Longmont, CO: Cambium Learning® Sopris.

Ebbers, S.M., and Denton, C.A. (2008). A root awakening: Vocabulary instruction for older students with reading difficulties. *Learning Disabilities Research and Practice, 23*(2), 90–102.

Edwards, E.C., Font, G., Baumann, J. F., and Boland, E. (2004). Unlocking word meanings: Strategies and guidelines for teaching morphemic and contextual analysis. In J. F. Baumann, and E. J. Kame'enui (eds.), *Vocabulary instruction: Research to practice* (pp. 159–176). New York: Guilford Press.

Ehrlich, I. (1968). *Instant Vocabulary*. New York: Pocket Books.

Frost, R. (2005). Orthographic systems and skilled word recognition processes in reading. In M. J. Snowling, and C. Hulme (eds.), *The science of reading: A handbook.* (pp. 272–295). Malden, MA: Blackwell Publishing.

Hendricks, R. (1992). *Latin made simple*. New York: Doubleday.

Henry, M.K. (2003). *Unlocking literacy: Effective decoding and spelling instruction*. Baltimore: Paul H. Brookes Publishing Co.

McBride-Chang, C., Wagner, R.K., Muse, A., Chow, B.W., and Shu, H. (2005). The role of morphological awareness in children's vocabulary acquisition in English. *Applied Psycholinguistics, 26,* 415–435.

Moats, L.C. (2000). *Speech to print: Language essentials for teachers*. Baltimore: Paul H. Brookes.

Nagy, W.E., and Anderson, R.C. (1984). How many words are there in printed school English? *Reading Research Quarterly, 19,* 304–330.

Nagy, W.E. (2007). Metalinguistic awareness and the vocabulary-comprehension connection. In R.K. Wagner, A.E Muse, and K.R. Tannenbaum (eds.), *Vocabulary acquisition: Implications for reading comprehension* (pp. 52–77). New York: Guilford Press.

Nurnberg, M., and Rosenblum, M.(1989). *How to build a better vocabulary*. New York: Warner Books.

Oxford English Dictionary. 2nd ed. (2002). CD-ROM. Oxford, UK: Oxford University Press.

Pinker, S. (1999). *Words and rules*. London: Weidenfeld and Nicolson.

Seymour, P.H.K. (2005). Early reading development in European orthographies. In M.J. Snowling, and C. Hulme (Eds.), *The science of reading: A handbook.* (pp. 296–315). Malden, MA: Blackwell Publishing.

Stahl, S.A. (1999). *Vocabulary development*. Newton Upper Falls, MA: Brookline Books.

Wolf, M. (2007). *Proust and the squid: The story and science of the reading brain*. New York: Harper.

DEAR SUBSTITUTE TEACHER
(A Letter to the Sub)

Dear Substitute Teacher,

Thank you for teaching in my absence. We have been learning about morphology. Morphology is the study of prefixes, suffixes, and roots (called morphemes). The book we use is called *Vocabulary Through Morphemes: Suffixes, Prefixes, and Roots for Intermediate and Secondary Grades.*

Please read and discuss page number _____ with the class. Let students have a minute or two to silently read the section. Then read the section aloud with the class, reading across each row. You read (modeling how to read it) and then the students echo what you read. Or, you read and stop partway, and students continue reading aloud, finishing the sentence.

As they read, students should look for morphemes they know. They should highlight or circle known base words and underline known suffixes and prefixes. For example, this is how the instructional page for the suffix *-y* should look after students have annotated it. The students have circled the base words and underlined the suffix *-y*.

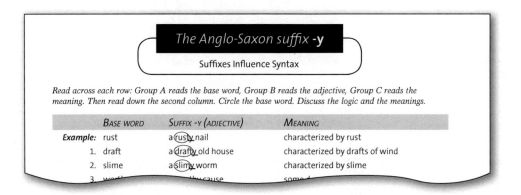

Each lesson has an instructional page on the left and a practice page on the right. The instructional page should only take about 15 minutes. Then let students complete the practice page; that should take about 10 minutes. First explain the examples, and make sure everyone knows how to do the assignment. Tell the students to answer the questions independently, alone. After they finish, encourage them to discuss their answers with a peer. (Throughout, the ✸ graphic indicates that students should read and discuss something with a partner.) Let them change their answers if they learn something new. In *Vocabulary Through Morphemes*, practice pages are not tests; they are part of the learning experience.

When everyone is finished, discuss the answers with the class. Answers are provided beginning on page 38 of the Teacher's Guide.

Thanks again! I hope you have a good day!

Quiz: Invaders of the English Language

Answer each question. Look back in prior pages for help.

1. The part I liked best in the history of the English language was when _____ (Answers will vary.) _____

2. The Romans spoke a language called _____ Latin _____ .

3. The Romans borrowed many words and ideas from the _____ Greeks _____ , including their mythological gods and goddesses.

4. The Romans colonized England for about __400__ years, until about 410.

5. The Anglo-Saxons spoke a _____ Germanic _____ language and had no alphabet.

6. The Anglo-Saxons treated the Celts very _____ unkindly, cruelly, unfairly, etc. _____ .

7. Scandinavian pirates, called Vikings, __ invaded or raided __ England, robbing and killing.

8. The Viking Danes and Norsemen raided for __>100__ years, until King Alfred brought peace.

9. Anglo-Saxons married Scandinavians; the differing Germanic languages blended or merged .

10. William the Conqueror invaded next, forcing the English to speak French or Norman-French .

11. French invaders married _____ English _____ women; the different languages blended.

12. Many French words came into English, including the word _____ (Answers will vary.) __ .

13. The French language is based on roots from the _____ Latin _____ language.

14. Most English words are Latin, French, Germanic, or _____ Greek _____ .

15. Every time England was _____ invaded _____ , the language changed.

16. During the Renaissance, English gained at least __10,000__ new words.

17. The Renaissance birthed many scientific words with _____ Greek _____ roots, like *telescope*.

18. Then England went to sea, colonizing distant lands like India and America. One word English adopted from the Native Americans (the Indians) is _____ (Answers will vary.) __ .

19. The English language ((is)) (is not) classified as a Germanic language.

20. English ((does)) (does not) contain a growing number of Spanish words.

21. The English language ((does)) (does not) contain a lot of synonyms.

22. English ((is)) (is not) still adopting new foreign words.

23. Many English words are formed with prefixes, roots, and _____ suffixes _____ (morphemes).

24. A morpheme contains clues about what a word _____ means _____ .

Compound Words

Part A: *Use morphemes from inside the compound word to complete each sentence.*

1. A *doorbell* is a type of _____ bell _____ .

2. A *red-winged blackbird* is a _____ blackbird _____ that has _____ red on its wings _____ .

3. A *blueberry* is a _____ berry _____ that is _____ blue _____ .

4. A *bottlenose dolphin* is a type of _____ dolphin _____ .

5. A *runaway train* is a train that is _____ out of control _____ .

6. *Kickboxing* is _____ a sport, boxing with feet instead of hands _____ .

7. *Skateboarding* is _____ a sport, riding a board with wheels _____ .

8. A *soccer mom* is _____ a female parent or guardian who supports soccer _____ .

9. A *jack-in-the-box* is _____ a toy, shaped like a box _____ .

Part B: *With a partner discuss each compound. Pretend you do not already know what the word means. Is the meaning literal or partly literal? Or is the meaning figurative? Do you need more context or a dictionary to understand it?*

Write **literal**, **figurative**, or **partly literal**:
(Answers will vary, but encourage critical thinking and reflective discussion.)

1. A *bulldozer* _____

2. Some *lipstick* _____

3. A *baseball glove* _____

4. A *sleepwalker* _____

5. A *polar ice cap* _____

6. A *jump rope* _____

7. Doing *cartwheels* _____

8. An *armchair* _____

9. A *traffic light* _____

10. An *egghead* _____

11. A *coffee cup* _____

12. A *movie star* _____

Part A: *The base word is* **act***, used as a verb in "We acted silly."*

1. Change *act* into a noun by adding a suffix: I'm a famous _____actor or actress_____ .

2. Transform *act* into an adjective: I see six _____active_____ children.

3. Change *act* into an adverb (attach two suffixes): We _____actively_____ protested.

Part B: *Write* **a verb, an adverb, a noun,** *or* **an adjective.** *Write the suffix that determined the word class.*

1. We *hope* it will rain. *Hope* is __a__ _____verb_____ . (no suffix; this is a base word)

2. We felt *hopeful*. *Hopeful* is __an__ _____adjective_____ . Suffix: __-ful__

3. We waited *hopefully* for news. *Hopefully* is __an__ _____adverb_____ . Suffix: _____-ly

4. We were filled with *hopefulness*. *Hopefulness* is __a__ _____noun_____ . Suffix: __-ness__

5. We are not *hopeless* people. *Hopeless* is __an__ _____adjective_____ . Suffix: _____-less

Part C: *Read the two morphological families of words. Circle the base in each word. Place an asterisk (*) by each compound word. Discuss word meanings with a partner.*

1.

(child)hood	(child)like	(child)ish	(child)ishness
(child)ishly	*(child) care	*step(child)	(child)ren

2.

(love)ly	(lov)ing	be(love)d	(lov)ingly
*tree-(love)r	(love)less	un(lov)ing	(love)able
*puppy (love)	*(love)sick	*(love) bug	*(love)birds

Part A: *Add the suffix -**y** to each base word to create a derivation.*
- If the word ends with an **e**, drop the **e** before adding the suffix **-y** (*nose* → *nosy*).
- If the word has one vowel and ends with one consonant, double the consonant before adding the suffix **-y** (*bat* → *batty*).

	Base	**Derivation (adjective)**
Example:	paste	pasty
1.	nut	nutty
2.	fog	foggy
3.	rose	rosy
4.	boss	bossy
5.	heart	hearty
6.	might	mighty
7.	scare	scary
8.	shine	shiny
9.	sun	sunny
10.	wrinkle	wrinkly
11.	shade	shady
12.	tingle	tingly
13.	grime	grimy
14.	grub	grubby
15.	simple	simply

Part B: *Respond to each question.*

1. What is the smallest possible base word in *pottery*? _pot_

2. Unscramble the morphemes **er** + **y** + **cover** + **dis**. _discovery_

The Anglo-Saxon suffixes -er and -est

Part A: *What does the suffix* **-er** *mean in each word and sentence? Check the correct column to show what the suffix* **-er** *denotes. Study the first three examples.*

	Target word	Contextualized use	(noun) 'One who'	(noun) 'That which'	(adjective) 'More'
Example:	stronger	This rope is stronger than that one.			✓
Example:	pitcher	Did the pitcher throw a fast ball?	✓		
Example:	toaster	Our toaster is broken.		✓	
1.	creamier	This milk is creamier than that milk.			✓
2.	catcher	The catcher caught the fly ball.	✓		
3.	stranger	I never saw a stranger-looking dog.			✓
4.	cooler	Put the water bottles in the cooler.		✓	
5.	mower	Use a lawnmower to cut the grass.		✓	
6.	heater	Did someone turn off the heater?		✓	
7.	dancer	Did a dancer leap across the stage?	✓		
8.	beater	We whip eggs with an egg beater.		✓	
9.	heavier	This rock is heavier than that one.			✓
10.	challenger	Did the challenger win the game?	✓		
11.	discoverer	A discoverer found the hidden cave.	✓		
12.	propeller	The propeller propels the plane.		✓	

Part B: *In the table below, does the target word end with the suffix* **-er**? *If yes, write the morphemic math as shown. Otherwise, place a check mark in one of the columns.*

	Target word	The suffix *-er*	No, not the suffix *-er*	I'm not sure
Example:	lovelier	love + -ly(i) + -er		
1.	her		✓	
2.	dodger	dodg¢ + er		
3.	healthier	health + y(i) + er		
4.	manager	manag¢ + er		
5.	weather		✓	
6.	containers	contain + er + s		

Vocabulary Through Morphemes / Suffixes

Practice Page / 23

The Anglo-Saxon suffix -ly

Part A: *Choose an adverb to complete each sentence. Write it. Several choices may apply.*

kindly	loudly	cruelly	proudly	quietly	intelligently
sisterly	honestly	patiently	suddenly	repeatedly	recently

Example: They waited _____ patiently / quietly _____ for their dinner.

1. Poor James shouted _____ loudly / repeatedly _____ for help.

2. Chad _____ kindly / repeatedly _____ fed the homeless, hungry cat.

3. Without warning, it _____ suddenly _____ began to rain hard.

4. He tiptoed _____ quietly _____ across the floor.

5. She _____ loudly / cruelly / repeatedly _____ blamed her brother for the accident.

6. "I _____ honestly _____ did not take it," insisted Fred.

7. She was _____ repeatedly / recently _____ warned to wear a helmet.

8. He _____ quietly / intelligently _____ reads the first chapter of his book.

9. We haven't seen that black dog _____ recently _____.

10. Dr. Jones answered each question _____ patiently / honestly / intelligently _____.

Part B: *For each adjective, change the final **y** to **i**, then add the suffix **-ly** to create an adverb.*

Example:	happy	happily
1.	hungry	hungrily
2.	hearty	heartily
3.	merry	merrily
4.	easy	easily

Part C: *Finish the table below.*

	Adjective	Phrase	Meaning of the phrase
Example:	sisterly	a *sisterly* hug	like a hug from a sister
1.	kingly	a *kingly* robe	like a robe a king wears
2.	neighborly	*neighborly* support	like support a neighbor gives
3.	friendly	a *friendly* greeting	like a greeting from a friend

The Anglo-Saxon suffix -hood

Morphotextual Mastery: *Read the passage several times, until fluent. Finish incomplete words by writing one suffix on the line. Read the sentence. Does it sound right? Does the whole story make sense? Read it aloud to a partner.*

Hummingbirds

There are few birds bright_er_ than a hummingbird when the sunlight strikes it. How it flashes as it flitters from one flower to another! It's a welcome guest in every yard and every neighbor_hood_

To attract hummingbirds to your home, feed them. Hang a feeding bottle secure_ly_ in the yard, far from cats and dogs. Use a bright red feeder because hummers are attracted to red. Fill the feeder with one-fourth cup of sugar entirely mixed into one cup of water. Do not use the powder_y_ kind of sugar. Fill the feeder on a week_ly_ basis, at least. Inspect the feeder periodical_ly_. Do not let black mold grow in it! Clean the feeder on a month_ly_ basis with bleach water, not with soap.

If you feed the winged beauty it will come. Suddenly it will dart into view. Stand back silent_ly_ and watch. Do not move or speak. Slowly, the hummer will become accustomed to you. Then it will trustingly approach the feeder even when you are nearby. A hummer will return repeated_ly_ to a feeder because it has the tiniest tummy. It must constantly refill it.

Use context clues and morpheme clues from the passage to answer the questions below.

1. Which **adverb** tells **how** the feeder should be hung? _____securely_____

2. Which **adverb** tells **how** to blend the water and sugar? _____entirely_____

3. Which **adjective describes** the type of sugar *not* to use? _____powdery_____

4. Which **adverb** tells **how often** the feeder should be refilled? _____weekly_____

5. **How often** should the feeder be cleaned? _____monthly_____

6. **How** will the hummer behave after it gets used to you? _____trustingly_____

7. **How often** will a hummingbird drink from the feeder? _repeatedly / constantly_

The Anglo-Saxon suffix -ful

Part A: *Read the phrase. Rewrite it as one word ending with the suffix* **-ful**. *If the word ends in* **y**, *change the final* **y** *to* **i** *before adding* **-ful**.

	Phrase with *full of*	Single word ending with *-ful*
Example:	full of pain	painful
1.	full of sorrow	sorrowful
2.	full of cheer	cheerful
3.	full of bliss	blissful
4.	full of grace	graceful
5.	full of regret	regretful
6.	full of pride	prideful
7.	full of joy	joyful
8.	full of peace	peaceful
9.	full of spite	spiteful
10.	full of beauty	beautiful
11.	full of plenty	plentiful
12.	full of mercy	merciful

Part B: *Add the suffix* **-ly** *to make an adverb. Write the adverb.*

Example: harmful   harmfully

1. vengeful   vengefully

2. scornful   scornfully

3. beautiful   beautifully

4. careful   carefully

5. thoughtful   thoughtfully

6. boastful   boastfully

7. full of power   powerfully

The Anglo-Saxon suffix -less

Part A: *Read the word. Write the opposite. Use the suffix* **-ful** *or* **-less** *in the word.*

Example: painful _____painless_____

Example: hopeless _____hopeful_____

1. fearful _____fearless_____

2. thoughtful _____thoughtless_____

3. helpful _____helpless_____

4. mindful _____mindless_____

5. successless _____successful_____

6. cheerless _____cheerful_____

7. joyful _____joyless_____

8. careless _____careful_____

9. faithless _____faithful_____

10. doubtful _____doubtless_____

11. pitiless _____pitiful_____

12. tasteless _____tasteful_____

13. powerful _____powerless_____

Part B: *Write the missing word. Add* **-fully** *or* **-lessly** *to the bracketed base word.*

1. Afraid to look down, they _____fearfully_____ climbed to the top of the cliff. [fear]

2. He _____heartlessly_____ threw the child's toy into the river. [heart]

3. He _____boastfully_____ showed everyone his perfect report card. [boast]

4. _____Mercifully_____, the dog was not left in the stifling-hot car. [Mercy]

The Latin suffixes -able and -ible

Morphotextual Mastery: *Skill-Builder: Finish each sentence by adding a logical suffix to the base word. Then read the sentence. Does it sound grammatically correct? Read each passage. Does each story make sense?*

1. That gentleman showed a great deal of honor when he was shopping at our jewelry store. In fact, he was quite honor___able___. He bought a ring. We mistaken___ly___ gave him too much change back, but he didn't keep it. He honorabl~~e~~___ly___ gave all of it back to us. We felt great___ly___ honored to meet him!

2. Can you afford to buy that used car? Is it afford___able___? Do you think it is the best deal? Is it the most affordabl~~e~~___ly___ priced car on the lot? Think careful___ly___ about it.

3. I learned about shooting stars recent___ly___. Last night, an astronomer told a remark___able___ story about stars. I want to learn more because shooting stars are marvel___ous___! Perhaps I will be a success___ful___ astronomer some day.

4. Before I play basketball, I start flexing my muscles. I bend and stretch until I feel very flex___ible___. When my muscles are limber, loose, and warmed up, I can flexibl~~e~~___ly___ touch my toes!

5. Beverly swam through the water as graceful___ly___ as a dolphin. She had been swimming all her life, since early child___hood___. She loved swim___ming___. Whenever she swam, she felt peace___ful___ and calm. If she ever had to stop swimming, she would feel great___ly___ disappointed.

BONUS ACTIVITY Multisensory, see page 97

Draw a picture and write a corresponding sentence for each of these phrases:

(Answers will vary.)

an ugsome creature	a nosy meddlesome friend

a heavy cumbersome load	a venturesome teenager

The Anglo-Saxon suffix -ish

Part A: *Decide how the target word is used in the sentence. Write* **adjective**, **verb**, *or* **adverb**.

	Target word	Used in a sentence (contextualized)	Part of speech
Example:	boyish	We like Sarah's new boyish haircut.	adjective
Example:	sluggishly	The car started sluggishly in the cold weather.	adverb
Example:	astonish	That trick will astonish the children.	verb
1.	feverishly	She worked feverishly to complete her report.	adverb
2.	cherish	Cherish the time spent with friends.	verb
3.	childish	The childish celebrity stamped her feet.	adjective
4.	elfish	Small and elfish, he crept across the room.	adjective
5.	publish	Our school will publish a newspaper.	verb
6.	stylishly	She dressed stylishly for her first day at work.	adverb
7.	foolishly	Martin foolishly wasted his money.	adverb
8.	accomplish	If we work we can accomplish our goal.	verb

Part B: *On each line, write the base word with the suffix attached, as described. Spell each derivation carefully. The first one is done for you.*

1. Change the word to an adjective. Double the final consonant, then add **-ish**:

   red ____reddish____   snob ____snobbish____

   pig ____piggish____   big ____biggish____

2. Change the word to an adjective. Drop the final silent **e**, then add **-ish**:

   blue ____bluish____   white ____whitish____   mule ____mulish____

   brute ____brutish____   purple ____purplish____   style ____stylish____

3. Change the word to an adverb by adding **-ish** + **-ly** (drop the final **e**, if applicable).

   self ____selfishly____   fool ____foolishly____

   mule ____mulishly____   rogue ____roguishly____

4. Change the word to an adjective. Write a word that ends with **-ish** to show nationality.

   Sweden ____Swedish____   England ____English____

   Spain ____Spanish____   Ireland ____Irish____

The Anglo-Saxon suffix -ness

Part A: *Write the base word(s) of the underlined derivation.*

Example: Look at the unusual <u>brightness</u> of that particular star. _____ bright _____

Example: Because of their <u>longearedness</u>, rabbits can hear well. _____ long + ear _____

1. The odd landscape filled us with a sense of <u>strangeness</u>. _____ strange _____

2. The miser was disliked for his <u>tightfistedness</u> and greed. _____ tight + fist _____

3. Eleanor Roosevelt was loved for her <u>kindheartedness</u>. _____ kind + heart _____

4. Suffering from <u>sleeplessness</u>, she counted sheep. _____ sleep _____

5. Did <u>carelessness</u> cause the great fire of Chicago? _____ care _____

6. We hire people characterized by <u>trustworthiness</u>. _____ trust + worth _____

7. Astronauts felt a sense of <u>weightlessness</u> on the moon. _____ weight _____

8. He talked on and on, until we tired of his <u>longwindedness</u>. _____ long + wind _____

Part B: *Reorder the scrambled morphemes. Write the whole word. Drop vowels and double consonants as needed to spell correctly.*

Example:	ness	ful	peace	peacefulness
1.	less	form	ness	formlessness
2.	help	ness	ful	helpfulness
3.	ness	thought	less	thoughtlessness
4.	ly	clown	ish	clownishly
5.	ly	pity	ful	pitifully

Part C: *Change the final* **y** *to an* **i**, *then add the suffix* **-ness** *to create an abstract noun.*

Example: lonely _____ loneliness _____

1. lovely _____ loveliness _____

2. kindly _____ kindliness _____

3. friendly _____ friendliness _____

The Latin suffix -cide

Part A: *For each word, what is being destroyed? Highlight the correct answer. The first one is done for you.*

1.	**suicide**	(one's self)	Sue
2.	**homicide**	a pig	(a human being)
3.	**fratricide**	a sister	(a brother)
4.	**infanticide**	(a baby)	a sports fan
5.	**ecocide**	(the environment)	noise
6.	**germicide**	Germans	(germs)
7.	**insecticide**	a culture	(insects)
8.	**regicide**	(a king or ruler)	a movie star
9.	**patricide**	(a father)	a mother
10.	**genocide**	Jean	(a whole ethnic race)

Part B: *Finish each sentence. Look at Part A above and review the opposite page.*

1. He is a homicidal maniac; we must stop him from _____killing_____ again.

2. When Julius Caesar was killed, it was a form of _____regicide_____.

3. A hospital uses germicidal cleansers to kill all the _____germs_____.

4. Farmers often spray _____insecticide_____ all over their crops, to kill all the insects.

Morphotextual Mastery: *Read the whole story. Finish incomplete words by writing one suffix on the line. Read the sentence. Does it sound right? Does the whole story make sense? Read again with fluency.*

Hummingbird Traps

A hummingbird was recently trapped in a garage in my neighbor _hood_ . The bird starved to death. Sadly, this has happened before. To understand how it happens, we must understand hummingbirds.

A hummingbird is small but superb_ ly _ built for flight. It is a super-speedy dynamo. Its wings move so rapidly they appear blurry. The fastest recorded wingbeat rate is 80 beats per second (not per minute, but per second). The wee wings hum like a well-oiled mini-motor. It takes energy to move. Energy comes from food. To fly so quickly, a hummer must eat frequent_ ly _. It cannot store food like bears do because its stomach is microsized. Hummingbirds must eat every 15 minutes in order to fly.

One of their favorite foods is the trumpet creeper flower. Hummingbirds are attracted to the bloom because it is red. Thirstily they sip the sugary nectar from the flower. They love nectar because of its sweet_ ness _. They notice the flower because it is so colorful. (Birds do not have a power _ful_ nose like dogs do, so they cannot smell the nectar from a distance.)

Hummers look for small red objects that look flower-ish. Most garage doors have a bright red emergency handle hanging from a cord. The small bright handle is clearly vis_ ible _. To a hummingbird, the handle looks a lot like a trumpet creeper flower. The hummer eagerly darts into the garage to inspect the "flower" and then it panics. Perhaps it thinks, "This flower is not edible! Is this some fiend_ ish _ trick?!" In panic, it flies up to the wooden rafters. Fear_ ful _ly confused, it freezes. It's stuck at the top of the garage without food! In only an hour, a hummingbird can starve to death.

Protect the hummingbirds (in Spanish, *los colibrises*). Guard them from garage-attack. This kind of avicide is prevent_ able _. Close the garage door. Do not be care_ less _ and leave it open all day. Polite_ ly _ ask your neighbors to keep their garage doors closed, too. Tell them about the red emergency handle. They will want to know, because everyone loves a hummer.

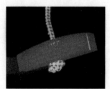

Part B: *There are some unusual or invented words and phrases in the hummingbird passage. Some are listed below. What do you think these words and phrases mean? Look in the story for help.*

1. In paragraph 2: a super-speedy dynamo   fast

2. In paragraph 2: its stomach is miscrosized   very tiny

3. In paragraph 2: hum like a well-oiled mini-motor   work smoothly

4. In paragraph 4: objects that look flower-ish   look like a flower

5. In paragraph 5: this kind of avicide   the act of killing birds

The Latin suffix -ment

Part A: *Write the correct word on the line. Choose words from below.*

predicament	judgment	astonishment	accomplishments
compartment	establishment	monument	announcements

1. The twins got into an awful _____predicament_____ at school.

2. Put the butter in the dairy _____compartment_____.

3. He was filled with _____astonishment_____ when he saw the alien spaceship.

4. Our library is an _____establishment_____ created for the benefit of the public.

5. Herman was proud of his daughter's musical _____accomplishments_____.

6. They constructed a granite _____monument_____ in his honor.

7. Tina shows good _____judgment_____ when she makes decisions.

8. We listened to the _____announcement_____ over the school intercom.

Part B: *Use sentence clues to fill in the blank with a word that ends with the suffix* **-ment**.

Example: We experience _____astonishment_____ when we feel astonished.

1. We feel a sense of _____accomplishment_____ when we accomplish difficult tasks.

2. We show good _____judgment_____ when we judge wisely.

3. We feel a sense of _____enjoyment_____ when we enjoy ourselves.

4. We feel _____amusement_____ when we are amused.

5. We take a _____measurement_____ when we measure something.

6. We add _____reinforcements_____ when we reinforce something.

BONUS ACTIVITY   **Multisensory, see page 99**

The Latin and Greek suffix -ic

Part A: *Rewrite the noun as an adjective by adding the suffix -ic.*

Example: hero _____ heroic _____

1. photon _____ photonic _____

2. electron _____ electronic _____

3. graph _____ graphic _____

4. telepath _____ telepathic _____

5. German _____ Germanic _____

Part B: *Morphotextual Mastery. Finish each sentence by adding a logical suffix to the base word. Read the sentence again. Does it sound grammatically correct? Read the story. Does it make sense? Read the passage several times, until fluent.*

Reading Log
I am reading a fantast_ic_ book about mythical beings. I read about some kind, helpful giants and some ug_ly_ (or ugsome) giants, too. There are horrible, terr_ible_ beasts that can suddenly turn invis_ible_. I meet graceful fairies and some elf_ish_ beings, too. My favorite character is the dragon_like_ being with four wings. I read this book for entertain_ment_ in my spare time. The plot is very interesting. Sometimes, I am filled with astonish_ment_ and amaze_ment_.

The Latin suffix -al

Part A: *For words that end with -ic, insert -al, then -ly to form an adverb. Write the adverb.*

	Ending with *-ic*	Adverb with *-al + -ly*
Example:	poetic	poetically
1.	music	musically
2.	dramatic	dramatically
3.	historic	historically
4.	athletic	athletically

Part B: *Circle one of the two words on the left to complete each sentence.*

essence	(essential)	Food is an _____ need.
substance	(substantial)	He has a _____ amount of money.
(circumstances)	circumstantial	We cannot judge her based on _____.
confidence	(confidential)	A counselor keeps everything _____.
(influence)	influential	That senator has a great deal of _____.
torrent	(torrential)	_____ rains caused catastrophic flooding.
office	(official)	Tina got an _____ membership card.
artifice	(artificial)	He has an _____ heart.
(finances)	financial	My bank handles _____.

Part C: *Write a base word for each derivative.*

	Derivative	Base word
Example:	burial	bury
1.	Oriental	Orient
2.	spherical	sphere
3.	denial	deny
4.	editorial	editor or edit
5.	original	origin

The Greek suffix -ist; the Latin suffixes -ian, -or

Part A: *Read the definition. Highlight the correct word for each one. Only one is correct.*

	Definition	-or	-ist	-(c) ian
1.	one who practices science	scienceor	(scientist)	sciencian
2.	one who practices music	musicor	musicist	(musician)
3.	one who practices biology	biologor	(biologist)	biologian
4.	one who professes	(professor)	professist	professian
5.	one who studies diets	dietor	dietist	(dietician)
6.	one who practices politics	politicor	politicist	(politician)
7.	one who educates	(educator)	educatist	educatian
8.	one who navigates	(navigator)	navigatist	navigatian
9.	one who donates	(donor)	donatist	donatian
10.	one who works in the Senate	(senator)	senatist	senatorian
11.	one who studies electricity	electricitor	electricitist	(electrician)
12.	one who studies history	historior	historist	(historian)
13.	one who studies library sciences	librarior	librarist	(librarian)

Part B: *Break the words down into base and suffixes.*

	Derivative	Base	Suffix	Suffix	Suffix	Suffix
Example:	athletically	athlete	-ic	-al	-ly	
1.	realistically	real	-ist	-ic	-al	-ly
2.	patriotically	patriot	-ic	-al	-ly	
3.	characteristically	character	-ist	-ic	-al	-ly

The Greek suffixes -ology, -ologist

 Work with a partner if preferable. Read the list of studies or professions.
- Place a check mark (✔) beside words that you know well.
- Place a question mark (?) beside words you know only minimally.
- Place a zero (0) by words you have never heard of or seen before.
- If you know one meaning of the word, but not as a "type of science," place a one (1) beside it.

(Answers will vary; no key.)

___ anthology	___ ethnology	___ phenomenology
___ anthropology	___ etymology	___ phonology
___ apology	___ geology	___ phraseology
___ archaeology	___ graphology	___ phrenology
___ archeology	___ ideology	___ physiology
___ astrology	___ meteorology	___ psychology
___ bacteriology	___ methodology	___ psychopathology
___ biology	___ microbiology	___ radiology
___ biotechnology	___ morphology	___ reflexology
___ cardiology	___ musicology	___ seismology
___ chronology	___ mythology	___ sociology
___ climatology	___ neurology	___ technology
___ cosmology	___ ophthalmology	___ terminology
___ criminology	___ ornithology	___ theology
___ dermatology	___ paleontology	___ toxicology
___ ecology	___ pathology	___ typology
___ embryology	___ pharmacology	___ zoology

BONUS ACTIVITY   **Multisensory, see page 101**

Vocabulary Through Morphemes / Suffixes

Practice Page / 53

The Germanic (Anglo-Saxon) suffix -ship

Challenge: *Sort the vocabulary words into the correct table, according to their meaning. Some answers may vary.*

leadership	membership	sportsmanship	governorship	hardship
readership	companionship	citizenship	relationship	scholarship
kingship	friendship	penmanship	horsemanship	marksmanship

art or skill of
leadership
sportsmanship
marksmanship
penmanship
horsemanship
scholarship*

a collective body or group
membership
readership
citizenship

a quality, state, or condition
hardship
companionship
relationship
scholarship*
friendship

rank, status, or office
governorship
kingship

* scholarship could go in either category

The Latin suffix -ous

Part A: *Reorder the scrambled word parts. Write the whole word. Drop vowels and double consonants as needed to spell correctly. Read the words aloud to a partner.*

Example:	-ness	-ous	joy	joyousness
1.	-ous	marvel	-ly	marvelously
2.	fame	-ly	-ous	famously
3.	-ous	danger	-ly	dangerously
4.	-ly	grieve	-ous	grievously
5.	-ship	govern	-or	governorship
6.	-ish	devil	-ly	devilishly
7.	-some	-ly	win	winsomely
8.	-ist	real	-ic	realistic
9.	-ic	simple	-ist	simplistic
10.	fool	-ly	-ish	foolishly
11.	-ly	-ous	courage	courageously
12.	-ful	-ly	faith	faithfully

Part B: *Read across each row. Highlight the correct word (or words) for each definition. Remember, the suffixes* **-ous** *and* **-ful** *each denote 'full of or having.'*

	Definition	Option A	Option B
1.	full of help	⟨'helpful'⟩	'helpous'
2.	full of pain	⟨'painful'⟩	'painous'
3.	full of danger	'dangerful'	⟨'dangerous'⟩
4.	full of scorn	⟨'scornful'⟩	'scornous'
5.	full of ridicule	'ridiculeful'	⟨'ridiculous'⟩
6.	full of trust	⟨'trustful'⟩	'trustous'
7.	full of joy	⟨'joyful'⟩	⟨'joyous'⟩
8.	full of grace	⟨'graceful'⟩	⟨'gracious'⟩

Part A: *Change the final* **y** *to an* **i***, then add the suffix* **-ous***.*

Example: envy   <u>envious</u>

1.   glory   <u>glorious</u>
2.   fury   <u>furious</u>
3.   victory   <u>victorious</u>
4.   mystery   <u>mysterious</u>
5.   vary   <u>various</u>

Part B: *Finish each analogy. Use words from the word bank.*

spacious	gracious	previous	splendiferous
contagious	delicious	anxious	treacherous

1. ***Gymnasium*** is to <u>spacious</u> as ***closet*** is to ***smallish***.

2. ***Pie*** is to <u>delicious</u> as ***pillow*** is to ***comfortable***.

3. ***Fire*** is to ***dangerous*** as ***influenza*** is to <u>contagious</u>.

4. ***Cowardly*** is to ***courageous*** as ***calm*** is to <u>anxious</u>.

5. ***Following*** is to <u>previous</u> as ***trusting*** is to ***suspicious***.

6. ***Wonderful*** is to <u>splendiferous</u> as ***terrible*** is to ***atrocious***.

7. ***Splendiferous*** is to ***splendor*** as <u>treacherous</u> is to ***treachery***.

For the target word, make a morpho-graphic poster showing colorful, stylistic word art. In the large box, write each morpheme in large print, using a different color or format for each one. In smaller print, label each prefix, base, or root with its meaning. Label the final suffix with the word class (noun, adjective, verb, or adverb). On the two lines below the box, use the word in a sentence. Share your creativity with others.

Example: creatively

create ('to make') + -ive ('tendency to') + -ly (adverb)

Target word: _____

(Answers will vary.)

_____

_____

The Latin suffix -age

Part A: *Use clues from the sentence to fill in the blank.*

Example: His **heir** will inherit a tremendous _____heritage_____.

1. Waste goes from the **sewer** to the _____sewage_____ plant.

2. Did the **orphan** live in an _____orphanage_____?

3. **Band** that wound with a _____bandage_____.

4. What are you **packing** into that _____package_____?

5. I cannot **steer**! My car has lost its _____steerage_____.

6. We'll drop **anchor** at a quiet _____anchorage_____.

7. **Pilgrims** went on a lengthy _____pilgrimage_____ to their holy land.

8. He was born into a **line** of kings; his _____lineage_____ is royal.

Part B: *Add the suffix to the base word. If necessary, change the final **y** to **i**, then add a suffix that begins with a vowel.*

Example:	glory + -ous	glorious
1.	acre + -age	acreage
2.	comfort + -able	comfortable
3.	optic + -ian	optician
4.	bother + -some	bothersome
5.	lug (g) + -age	luggage
6.	marry + -age	marriage
7.	carry + -age	carriage
8.	line + -age	lineage
9.	angel + -ic	angelic
10.	patriot + -ic + -al + -ly	patriotically
11.	fury + -ous	furious
12.	vary + -ous	various

The Latin suffix -ant

Circle or highlight each word that ends with the suffix -ant. Decide if it is used as an adjective or a noun. Study the examples before beginning. Remember, a **noun** is a person, place, thing, idea, or feeling. An **adjective** describes a noun.

Example: Gasping for breath, Todd reached for his (inhalant).

_____ noun

Example: Jennifer was clothed in a (brilliant) blue dress.

_____ adjective

1. The (defendant) approached the bench.

_____ noun

2. One (valiant) ant defended his home against invading termites.

_____ adjective

3. Tomás and Pedro enjoyed a (pleasant) day at the park.

_____ adjective

4. Dr. Early looked (elegant) in his new suit.

_____ adjective

5. Our flight (attendant) pointed out the emergency exits.

_____ noun

6. Can the speech (consultant) help Timmy learn to speak?

_____ noun

7. Iris was (reluctant) to study for her test.

_____ adjective

8. Stubbornly (defiant) Pat refused to go to school.

_____ adjective

9. Five angry, (militant) mothers protested against drunk driving.

_____ adjective

10. That raft floats well; it is very (buoyant) like a buoy.

_____ adjective

11. That frog is a (mutant); it has gone through a transformation.

_____ noun

12. "My dog is (pregnant)," Nina shouted with surprise.

_____ adjective

The Latin suffix -ent

Morphotextual Mastery: *Read the whole story, silently. Then work with a partner. Finish incomplete words by writing one suffix on the line. Read the sentence. Does it sound right? Read the whole story again, aloud, with fluency.*

Legendary Gods of Old England

The historic time period known as Old English began approximate_ly_ 1,500 years ago. This was the time of the Germanic Anglo-Saxons and the Scandinavian Vikings. The Anglo-Saxons and Vikings were superstitious and imaginative. They told many wonder_ful_ stories to explain their world. What did these people believe? Who were their gods?

One of their mythical gods was called Thunor, also known as Thor, the god of the sky. Thor was a benevolent, kind god. The Vikings were depend_ent_ (or ant) on Thor. They believed that Thor was protect_ive_ of them, especially during storms. Thunder boomed when Thor threw his marvel_ous_ hammer at enemies in the sky. Hot lightning sizzled. To the Vikings, it was transparent_ly_ clear that Thor existed—the proof was in his thunderous lightning. A scientific explanation for the storm was simply unaccept_able_.

The Anglo-Saxons prayed to Woden, the god of the ancient Germans. Woden was the most power_ful_ god of the whole Germanic race. The Anglo-Saxons believed that Woden guided them to England and helped them take the fertile land from the Celts. Historical_ly_, Germanic chieftains claimed that their lineage could be traced back to Woden. They claimed that their herit_age_ was royal and god-given.

The Anglo-Saxons also believed that lesser gods filled the environ_ment_. The lesser gods were elves, dwarfs, fairies, dragons, and ug_some_ (or ly) ogres. In the old tales, some magic_al_ beings were benevolent, like the friendly fairies. Others were danger_ous_. For example, according to legend, vicious elves shot poison_ous_ arrows called "elfshot" at humans.

Today, fairy tales are told in many differ_ent_ languages. Some Old English myths have been made into movies, including the unforget(t)able story of *Beowulf*. We enjoy these wondrous legends, but we know elves and fairies are nonexist_ent_. Right?

BONUS ACTIVITY Multisensory, see page 103

Assessment: Midway Review

Write each word as a morphological math statement, as shown. Write the grammatical function (noun, verb, adjective, adverb).

Example: reliably — rely + able + ly → reliably (adverb)

Example: sleepiness — sleep + y + ness → sleepiness (noun)

Example: dreamy — dream + y → dreamy (adjective)

1. hungrier — hungry + er (adjective)
2. acceptable — accept + able (adjective)
3. childishly — child + ish + ly (adjective)
4. historian — history + ian (noun)
5. enlargement — enlarge + ment (noun)
6. blissfully — bliss + ful + ly (adverb)
7. abusively — abuse + ive + ly (adverb)
8. anchorage — anchor + age (noun)
9. defiantly — defy + ant + ly (adverb)
10. creatively — create + ive + ly (adverb)
11. irksome — irk + some (adjective)
12. attendant — attend + ant (noun)
13. contentment — content + ment (noun)

General Review and Assessment: Morphological Families

In each row, which word does not belong? Circle the word that is not part of the morphological family. If all the words do belong together, write **all fit**. *Before beginning, study the two examples.*

Example:	cloud	cloudy	(loud)	cloudier	_____
Example:	sand	sandbox	sandy	sandier	_all fit_
1.	cartoon	(car)	cartoonish	cartoonist	_____
2.	reptile	reptilian	reptiles	(tiles)	_____
3.	green	greener	greenery	greenhouse	_all fit_
4.	(off)	office	officer	official	_____
5.	(luck)	reluctant	reluctantly	reluctance	_____
6.	farm	farmer	farmyard	(far)	farming	_____
7.	depend	dependable	dependent	(deepen)	depending	_____
8.	please	(lease)	pleasant	pleasing	pleasantly	_____
9.	quick	quicken	quickly	quicksand	(quit)	_____
10.	habit	(bit)	habitat	habitual	habitually	_____
11.	sun	sunny	sunnier	(sunken)	sunshine	_____
12.	establish	stable	(estimate)	establishing	establishment	_____
13.	act	active	actress	actor	actively	_all fit_

The Latin suffix -ance, -ence

Part A: *Finish each analogy. Use words found in the word bank. Work with a partner if preferable.*

brilliance	admittance	defiance
intelligence	auditorium	assistance

1. **Resistance** is to _____ defiance _____ as **confidence** is to **assurance**.

2. **Good Samaritan** is to _____ assistance _____ as **enemy** is to **harm**.

3. **Rocks** are to _____ intelligence _____ as **pigs** are to **wings**.

4. **Ticket** is to _____ admittance _____ as **egg** is to **omelet**.

5. **Audience** is to _____ auditorium _____ as **patients** are to **hospital**.

6. **Sun** is to _____ brilliance _____ as **cave** is to **darkness**.

Part B: *Use sentence clues to finish each statement with a word ending with **-ence** or **-ance**.*

Example: One who *tolerates* differences has the quality of _____ tolerance _____.

1. One who is *innocent* has the quality of _____ innocence _____.

2. One who is *accepted* is in a state of _____ acceptance _____.

3. One who is *patient* has the characteristic of _____ patience _____.

4. One who is *assured* has the characteristic of _____ assurance _____.

5. One who is *extravagant* has the characteristic of _____ extravagance _____.

6. One who is *elegant* has the characteristic of _____ elegance _____.

7. One who is *confident* has the characteristic of _____ confidence _____.

8. That which *occurs* is an _____ occurrence _____.

9. When two or more groups become *allies*, they form an _____ alliance _____.

The Latin suffix **-ary**

Fill in the blank with a word from the word bank.

infirmary	summary	obituary	dictionary
statuary	mortuary	granary	library

1. Get some grain from the _____ granary _____.

2. View the sculptures and statues in that group of _____ statuary _____.

3. A _____ dictionary _____ will tell you how to pronounce a word with correct diction.

4. Find books and information in the public _____ library _____.

5. Read about his death in the _____ obituary _____ section of the newspaper.

6. Visit sick and infirm people at an _____ infirmary _____.

7. Pay your respects at the _____ mortuary _____, or funeral home.

8. Read the main points in a short _____ summary _____ of the book.

Part A: *Read each sentence. On the line, write* **noun**, **verb**, **adjective**, *or* **adverb**.

Example: I see an **image** of a rabbit in that cloud. _____noun_____

1.   Try to **imagine** a world without war or poverty. _____verb_____

2.   The child plays with an **imaginary** friend. _____adjective_____

3.   J. K Rowling, a famous author, has a vivid **imagination**. _____noun_____

4.   An **imaginative** thinker could turn this empty lot into a marvelous garden. _____adjective_____

5.   Thinking **imaginatively**, she sculpted the ice into the shape of a dolphin. _____adverb_____

6.   We saw every kind of animal **imaginable** at the zoo today. _____adjective_____

7.   Vivid, colorful words created a strong sense of **imagery** in my poem. _____noun_____

 Part B: *Read each word. Highlight or circle the words that name places or things. Leave the adjectives blank. Look back in the book or refer to a dictionary for help.*

temporary	imaginary	primary	sanitary
(creamery)	(fishery)	legendary	secondary
(granary)	(statuary)	necessary	(infirmary)
(bestiary)	(obituary)	(topiary)	tertiary
military	extraordinary	ordinary	cautionary
honorary	voluntary	(sanctuary)	hereditary
(boundary)	(mortuary)	complimentary	(livery)

The Latin suffix -ize (from Greek -izein)

Read the sentences in each passage. Write the grammatical function (word class) of the boldface word. Refer to the box below for help deciding the class.

Grammatical function, word class			
Noun who, what	**Adjective** describes noun	**Verb** the action	**Adverb (-ly)** how the verb is done

Passage 1 *Andy the Actor*		Word class
Example	Andy liked *drama*, so he joined the theater club.	noun
1.	He had always been a very *dramatic* fellow.	adjective
2.	He liked to *dramatize* his own stories and write his own skits.	verb
3.	Sometimes he *dramatically* acted out his skits for his parents.	adverb
4.	Andy especially liked the *dramatic* endings.	adjective
5.	He couldn't wait for the *dramatization* of Scrooge.	noun

Passage 2 *Thaddeus the Thinker*		Word class
1.	Thaddeus had not always had a good *memory*.	noun
2.	There was a time when *memorization* was difficult for him.	noun
3.	It was nearly impossible for Thad to *memorize* his math facts.	verb
4.	Then he learned a new trick to improve his *memory*.	noun
5.	It was a *memorable* day for Thaddeus when that happened.	adjective

Passage 3 *Kasheena the Leader*		Word class
1.	Many students wanted to *form* a student council at school.	verb
2.	The principal *formalized* the application procedure.	verb
3.	A *formal* announcement went out to the school.	adjective
4.	Several students *formally* applied for the position.	adverb
5.	Kasheena *formulated* a plan. Her election campaign was dynamite. Kasheena won the most votes!	verb

For each word write the base word as shown in the examples.

Example:	reliably	rely
Example:	sleepiness	sleep
Example:	famous	fame
1.	dreamy	dream
2.	moisture	moist
3.	hungriest	hungry or hunger
4.	acceptable	accept
5.	childishness	child
6.	historian	history
7.	commitment	commit
8.	emperorship	emperor
9.	anchorage	anchor
10.	troublesome	trouble
11.	blissfully	bliss
12.	glorious	glory
13.	attendant	attend
14.	contentment	content
15.	healthy	health
16.	pianist	piano
17.	characteristically	character
18.	pleasurable	pleasure or please
19.	cautionary	caution
20.	creature	create
21.	legendary	legend
22.	resident	reside
23.	confidant	confide

BONUS ACTIVITY   **Multisensory, see page 105**

The Latin suffix -ate

Place a check to show how the target word is used in each phrase below. Is the target word used as a verb or an adjective? Say the word aloud. Listen. How is the suffix pronounced?

Phrase with target word in bold type	Target word class		How to say the suffix	
	Vb.	Adj.	/āte/	/uht/
1. **separate** the quarrelsome dogs	✓		✓	
2. slowly **calculate** the total	✓		✓	
3. is incredibly **articulate**		✓		✓
4. is **fortunate** or lucky or blessed		✓		✓
5. an **accurate** statement		✓		✓
6. **activate** all the robots	✓		✓	
7. **create** with imagination	✓		✓	
8. a **literate** speaker		✓		✓
9. will **emancipate** every slave	✓		✓	
10. only an **estimate**, not exact		✓		✓
11. too **delicate** for young children		✓		✓
12. do not **abbreviate** any words	✓		✓	
13. **navigate** the entire globe	✓		✓	
14. did not clearly **communicate**	✓		✓	
15. so very **unfortunate**		✓		✓
16. **contemplate**, then speak	✓		✓	
17. an **adequate** amount of rainfall		✓		✓
18. finally was able to **locate**	✓		✓	

Phrase with target word in bold type	Target word class		How to say the suffix	
	Vb.	Adj.	/āte/	/uht/
19. a **delicate** ornament		✓		✓
20. will very quickly **evaporate**	✓		✓	
21. **congratulate** you and your family	✓		✓	
22. for miles they **migrate**	✓		✓	
23. **devastate** the countryside	✓		✓	
24. can **demonstrate** how it works	✓		✓	
25. a **passionate** reader		✓		✓
26. **moderate**, mild weather		✓		✓
27. the **ultimate** driving machine		✓		✓
28. the **appropriate** clothing		✓		✓
29. an **articulate** speaker		✓		✓
30. can **educate** a monkey	✓		✓	
31. so **congratulate** the hardest worker	✓		✓	
32. **fascinate** the curious cat	✓		✓	
33. a **considerate** fellow, thoughtful		✓		✓
34. did not **frustrate** us at all	✓		✓	
35. would suddenly **operate**	✓		✓	
36. can **eliminate** two answers	✓		✓	

The Latin suffix -ion (-sion, -tion)

Choose a word from the bank to complete the sentence. Write the word on the line.

mission	profession	destruction	rotation
intermission	compassion	confession	collection
hibernation	inspiration	exaggeration	inspection

Example: I have a large _____collection_____ of baseball cards.

1. Hear my _____confession_____: I took the cookies from the cookie jar!

2. It was an _____exaggeration_____ when we said we caught 42 fish.

3. Several astronauts went on a space _____mission_____ to Mars.

4. War always ends in death and _____destruction_____.

5. Bears go into _____hibernation_____ during the winter.

6. The _____rotation_____ of the earth causes daylight and night

7. During _____intermission_____, we will go get some water.

8. Dr. Dart enjoys being a member of the medical _____profession_____.

9. We felt sympathy and _____compassion_____ for the suffering horse.

10. The beauty of nature always fills me with _____inspiration_____.

11. The criminologist conducted an _____inspection_____ at the scene of the crime.

The Latin suffix combination -ation

Part A: *Finish each framed sentence. Write a word that ends with the suffix* **-ion**. *Use clues from the sentence.*

Example: _____ Invasion _____ occurs when we *invade* another's territory.

1. _____ Division _____ occurs when we *divide* things.

2. A _____ decision _____ is reached when people *decide* something.

3. A _____ collision _____ occurs when two cars *collide*.

4. A _____ conclusion _____ is reached when we *conclude*, or come to the end.

5. Programs are *televised* so people can watch them on the _____ television _____.

6. _____ Confusion _____ occurs when people feel *confused*.

7. _____ Participation _____ occurs when people *participate*, or join in.

8. A _____ demonstration _____ takes place when someone *demonstrates* something.

9. _____ Hibernation _____ occurs when bears *hibernate*, or sleep, through the winter.

10. One experiences _____ alienation _____ when one feels like a stranger, like an *alien*.

Part B: *Rewrite each noun as an adjective that ends with the suffix* **-able** *or* **-ible**. *TIP: Nouns that end with* **-ation** *can be changed into adjectives that end with* **-able**.

Example: consideration _____ considerable _____

1. vegetation _____ vegetable _____

2. collection _____ collectible or collectable _____

3. division _____ divisible _____

4. permission _____ permissible _____

The Latin suffix -ity

Part A: *For each word, write one or two related words.* (Answers will vary; some are provided here.)

Example: hostility _____hostile, hostage_____

1. ability _____able, disability, capability_____

2. fragility _____fragile_____

3. purity _____pure, purify, purification, etc._____

4. intensity _____intense, intensification, intensify_____

5. possibility _____possible, impossible_____

6. security _____secure, securely_____

7. reality _____real, unreal_____

8. probability _____probably, probable, improbable_____

9. superiority _____super, superior_____

10. simplicity _____simple, simplistic, simplistically_____

Part B: *For each definition, write a word ending with* **-ity***.*

Example: state of being able _____ability_____

1. quality of being real _____reality_____

2. state of being pure _____purity_____

3. state of being curious _____curiosity_____

4. state of being dignified _____dignity_____

5. state of being sincere _____sincerity_____

The Latin suffix -tude

Morphotextual Mastery: *Read the entire passage. Then, highlight and paraphrase all the words that end with the suffix* **-tude***. To do so, examine the context and the morphemes. Retell the story to a partner. Read again with fluency.*

Sailing Alone Across the Sea

Sailing had always come easily to Dean. In fact, he had an aptitude for the sport. He understood wind direction, the flow of the currents, and the changing tides. He knew how to hoist the sails and lower them too. Dropping an anchor was not difficult for Dean either. In fact, he felt completely confident about sailing. Dean's main ambition was to sail on an extended voyage, alone. He wanted to single-handedly sail across the sea. With certitude, he knew he was ready for the challenge.

Dean began planning for his long-distance voyage. He planned carefully, with exactitude. Everything had to be just right. First, he plotted his course, using his navigational charts to find latitude and longitude. Then he checked that his rigging was in good condition. He listened to a reliable meteorologist, checking the long-range weather reports. As the big day approached, he stocked his kitchenette with an abundant supply of food and water. He was ready for departure.

Finally, Dean began his journey, sailing due east. At first, Dean was ecstatic. What an adventure! He was finally achieving a lifetime dream. Each day he thrilled at the marvelous splendor of the sea. Each night he counted a multitude of stars, feeling amazed at their brilliant magnitude. Dean felt fearless, strong, and courageous. Filled with fortitude, he sailed onward, alone.

His attitude remained positive and upbeat for a long while. Then reality began to set in. He was alone in the middle of the ocean with absolutely no one in sight. He had been on his sailboat for a month. The solitude was driving him crazy. The quietude was getting on his nerves. Dean needed human interaction. He was very tired of his own company.

With gratitude, Dean finally observed another boat on the distant horizon. He shouted with joy. To ensure that the approaching crew saw him, he hoisted a brightly colored flag. With relief he saw the crew on the other boat hoist a similar flag. They saw him! They were changing course and sailing directly toward him now! Dean's lonely period of solitude was about to end.

Part A: *Fill in the blank cell with a related derivative that ends with the suffix -istic.*

	-ism	-istic
Example:	legalism	legalistic
1.	realism	realistic
2.	feudalism	feudalistic
3.	communism	communistic
4.	pessimism	pessimistic
5.	optimism	optimistic

Part B: *Fill in the blank with the missing derivative or derivatives.*

	-ism	-istic	-istically
Example:	legalism	legalistic	legalistically
1.	realism	realistic	realistically
2.	chauvinism	chauvinistic	chauvinistically
3.	fatalism	fatalistic	fatalistically
4.	pessimism	pessimistic	pessimistically
5.	optimism	optimistic	optimistically

Part C: *Analogies. Circle the correct word to complete the analogy.*

- ***King*** is to (monarchism, Catholicism) as ***chief*** is to ***tribalism.***

- ***Prejudice*** is to (racism, alcoholism) as ***tolerance*** is to ***pluralism.***

- ***Paul Revere*** is to ***patriotism*** as (Babe Ruth, George Lucas) is to ***athleticism.***

- ***Pessimistic*** is to ***Eeore*** as (optimistic, artistic) is to ***Pooh Bear.***

Morphotextual Mastery: *Read the whole story. Finish incomplete words by writing one suffix on the line. Read the sentence. Does it sound right? Does the story make sense? Read aloud with fluency.*

Remnants of the Roman Empire

Once upon a time, only 2,000 years ago, the city of Rome (in Italy) was the capital of the gigantic Roman Empire. Power_ful_ Roman emperors ruled a large part of old Europe, including France, Spain, and England. These Romans were ancient Italians, from Italy.

Today, the Roman Empire is nonexist_ent_. The Roman Empire came crashing down when invaders ferocious_ly_ stormed into Rome. In the year 410 Rome "fell" into enemy hands. With their capital city under attack, Roman soldiers from all over Europe rushed fear_ful_ly back home to Rome to defend their turf from the destruct_ive_ raiders. Alas! It was not to be. The Roman Empire eventually fell entirely, and it did not rise again. However, many Roman stories have survived. The Romans spoke Latin. Speaking Latin, they told many tales, called legends or myths.

The most famous Roman legend begins with Mars, the god of war (a planet was named after him). According to the myth, Mars fell in love with a human. Nine months later, twins were born. The babies were semi-gods named Romulus and Remus. Everyone expected the children of Mars to become great and might_y_. Romulus and Remus were royal children. The kingdom was their rightful inherit_ance_.

A jealous uncle wanted the throne, so he carried the babes deep into the woods. There, he piti_less_ly left them to die. A protective she-wolf found Romulus and Remus. She fed them and raised them to adult_hood_. As adults, they courageous_ly_ fought their greedy uncle. Romulus and Remus were triumph_ant_; they won the battle. The twins claimed ownership of their stolen king_hood_ *(or ship)*. Remus eventually died. Romulus built the marvel_ous_ city of Rome, right on top of a hill. Rome was named after Romulus—a babe who was the legend_ary_ son of Mars, the god of war—a babe who was raised in the forest by a she-wolf.

Italia
(Italy)

ROMA

The fantastical legend of Romulus and Remus is the great_est_ of all the Roman myths. The story has not changed in over 2,000 years; it is consist_ent_ly the same. Some credible historians believe that parts of the story are factual, not fictitious. Other knowledge_able_ experts claim that the whole tale is unrealist_ic_. The facts are debatable but the story is frequently told, perhaps because it is mysterious. Italians today love to tell the story: A babe who spent his child_hood_ in the wilder_ness_ became the found_er_ of Rome.

The monument_al_ Roman Empire is gone. The Romans are gone. But the stories they told in Latin are not gone. The planets they named after their mythologic_al_ gods are not gone. The roots of their Latin language are not gone. If you speak Italian, Spanish, Portuguese, or French, you speak a "romance" language made of Latin roots. If you speak English well, approximate_ly_ half the words you know flow from Latin. These leftover pieces of history might be called "the remnants of Rome."

Cumulative Assessment

*Write the base word for each derivation. Write the grammatical function (**noun, verb, adjective, adverb**) of the whole word (not the base word). Before beginning, study the examples.*

Word	Grammatical function	Base
Example: governorship	noun	govern
Example: studiously	adverb	study
1. loveliness	noun	love
2. fortunately	adverb	fortune
3. carriage	noun	carry
4. invitation	noun	invite
5. sponsorship	noun	sponsor
6. fossilization	noun	fossil
7. endurance	noun	endure
8. pleasantly	adverb	pleasant or please
9. professionalism	noun	profess or profession
10. monarchism	noun	monarch
11. personality	noun	person
12. communicatively	adverb	communicate
13. humorously	adverb	humor
14. anchorages	noun	anchor
15. characteristically	adverb	character
16. measurable	adjective	measure
17. glamorousness	noun	glamour or glamor
18. plentitude	noun	plenty
19. fatality	noun	fatal
20. superiority	noun	super

Assessment: Suffixes Influence Syntax

Assessment: Suffixes Influence Syntax

Choose the grammatically correct word for the blank line. Circle it.

Example:	It's a ____ day.	newly	newness	newest	(new)
1.	What a ____ cat!	protection	(protective)	protect	protectively
2.	Which lamp is ___?	(brightest)	brightly	brighten	brights
3.	The pig is ____.	slop	(sloppy)	sloppiness	slopped
4.	What a ____ song!	joy	enjoyment	(joyous)	joyfully
5.	We felt a ____.	sensible	senses	sensitively	(sensation)
6.	I am an ____ person.	action	(active)	activation	activity
7.	We ate ____.	hunger	hungering	hungered	(hungrily)
8.	I can ____ the clock.	operation	operator	operative	(operate)
9.	It's a ____ of birds.	multiply	multiples	(multitude)	multiplication
10.	I visited the ____.	national	(nation)	nationality	nationhood
11.	What a ___ dog!	loudest	loudly	loudness	(loud)
12.	I giggled in my ____.	children	childish	childishly	(childhood)
13.	I will ___ my project.	final	finality	finally	(finalize)
14.	We study ____.	tribe	tribal	(tribalism)	tribalistic
15.	This test was ____.	funnest	funner	(fun)	funning

Part A: *Morphotextual Mastery. Read the passage silently. Write a prefix on the line to complete the unfinished words. Circle or highlight all words that begin with the prefix* **re-**. *Summarize main ideas to a partner. Read the passage aloud to develop fluency.*

Revival Park

(Revival) Park was not a welcoming place. No flowers bloomed. No grass grew. The park was filled with rubbish. Bottles, cans, and newspapers littered the ground. Broken glass slivered the sidewalk. Every bench and table was broken. This park was not the place to go for __re__ creation. The neighborhood children had no safe park in which to play. The Jacksons decided to do something about that. Katrina and Ken called all the neighbors together for a meeting. "We need to (renew) this old park," they told the neighbors. "We need to (restore) it and __re__ build it. If we all work together, we can (reclaim) this property for our children."

The neighborhood thought it was a good idea. They all got busy. The children filled their sacks with rubbish from the old park. They took six sacks of aluminum cans to the __re__ cycling center. Newspaper (reporters) came to see what was happening. They took photographs and wrote articles for the paper. The whole town read about the rebirth of (Revival) Park. Volunteers from all over town offered to help the neighbors __re__ claim their play place. Men with cement trucks offered to (resurface) the cracked sidewalks. Volunteers with lumber and nails offered to (rebuild) the broken benches. Children offered to __re__ plant the flower beds and (reseed) the grass. Nearly everyone in the city helped __re__ store the park to its former glory. The (restoration) of (Revival) Park was a community project.

Part B: *Add the prefix* **re-** *to each word. Do not add or drop any other letters. Think about the meanings of the two words. Write whether or not they are opposites. A dictionary is helpful.*

	Add the prefix *re-*	Opposite in meaning?
Example: turning	returning	no, not usually
1. appear	reappear	yes, usually
2. bound	rebound	no, not usually
3. calculate	recalculate	yes
4. cover	recover	no, not usually
5. enter	reenter	yes
6. serve	reserve	no, not usually

Part A: *Write the opposite for each word. Before beginning, study the examples.*

Example:	unkind	kind
Example:	able	unable
1.	uncomfortable	comfortable
2.	unchanging	changing
3.	unpolluted	polluted
4.	unfeeling	feeling
5.	unbreakable	breakable
6.	uneducated	educated
7.	unbeatable	beatable
8.	uncivil	civil
9.	unworthy	worthy
10.	unlikely	likely

Part B: *Respond to each question. Write an answer on each line.*

1. The old word *kempt* has faded from existence, but *unkempt* is still used today. The opposite of *unkempt* is not *kempt*. What does *unkempt* mean?

   messy, ungroomed, dirty, unwashed (not kept up)

   For further study, read the word origins for *unkempt* at www.etymonline.com. Type *unkempt* into the search field. In what year did *unkempt* first appear in written documents?

   about 1570

2. The opposite of *uneasy* is not *easy*. What does *uneasy* mean?

   a bit uptight, nervous, feeling like something is wrong

3. Name a word that is nearly the opposite of *uneasy*:

   confident, secure, at ease, relaxed, trusting

BONUS ACTIVITY Multisensory, see page 163

The Latin prefix in-

Part A: *For each word, write the opposite or near opposite (antonym) on the line. Begin each word with the prefix* **in-** *(also spelled* **im-**, **il-**, **ir-***).*

Example:	voluntary	involuntary
1.	possible	impossible
2.	logical	illogical
3.	capable	incapable
4.	edible	inedible
5.	credible	incredible
6.	human	inhuman
7.	dependent	independent
8.	patient	impatient
9.	responsible	irresponsible
10.	curable	incurable
11.	legible	illegible
12.	regular	irregular
13.	sensitive	insensitive
14.	correct	incorrect
15.	equality	inequality
16.	active	inactive
17.	legal	illegal

Part B: *Morphotextual Mastery. The prefix* **in-** *can mean 'not' but it can also mean 'in.' In the passage below, circle the boldface words where the prefix* **in-** *means 'in' as in* **intake***.*

Eagles are proud and ***independent*** birds. They **inhabit** high places, like mountaintops, building large nests in ***inaccessible*** locations that can only be reached by flight. Sitting high up on their lofty aerie, these raptors can see for miles. With eagle-eye vision, they scan the territory below, always keeping guard against ***intruders*** or ***invaders*** and always on the lookout for prey.

Fill in the blank with a word from the word bank.

noncommittal	noninvasive	nondescript	contradict
counterproductive	counterfeit	contraband	nonprofit
contraceptive	contrast	contrary	counterclockwise

1. _____ Contrary _____ to opinion at the time, Galileo claimed that the earth revolved around the sun.

2. His version of the facts may _____ contradict _____ your version.

3. A _____ contraceptive _____ is used to prevent birth.

4. The smuggler is carrying _____ contraband _____ guns.

5. _____ Contrast _____ a cat and a dog; they differ in several ways.

6. A library is a _____ nonprofit _____ organization, not a money-making business.

7. The car was plain and ordinary, quite _____ nondescript _____.

8. His shrug was _____ noncommittal _____, an indication that he was making no commitments.

9. Laser surgery is quick and _____ noninvasive _____

10. Several students ran around the track in a _____ counterclockwise _____ direction.

11. The _____ counterfeit _____ bills were illegally produced in a basement.

12. Farmers know it is _____ counterproductive _____ to let the cows roam in the corn.

The Latin prefixes **anti-** and **dis-**

Fill in the blank with a word from the word bank.

antiseptic	disembark	disadvantage	antipathy
antifreeze	disenchantment	antinuclear	dismissively
antisocial	antibiotics	disembodied	dismantled
disguise	antonyms	disintegrate	

1. The doctor prescribed _____ antibiotics _____ to help the patient fight against the virus.

2. Use _____ antifreeze _____ to keep your engine's water from freezing.

3. Numerous _____ antinuclear _____ activists protested outside the nuclear power plant.

4. The victim felt the deepest _____ antipathy _____ toward his attackers; he loathed them.

5. Use an _____ antiseptic _____ cream on that wound; it will kill all the germs.

6. Life and death are _____ antonyms _____, words of opposing meaning, yet they are related.

7. One may be classified as _____ antisocial _____ for abusing people or animals.

8. The Statue of Liberty was constructed in France, _____ dismantled _____ for packing and transportation to America, and then reconstructed in New York.

9. One _____ disadvantage _____ to living in Hawaii is the constant rainfall.

10. After the war, the soldier knew only _____ disenchantment _____ and despair.

11. After several years in the sun, the thin plastic will _____ disintegrate _____ into little shards.

12. After weeks at sea, the crew was happy to _____ disembark _____.

13. The _____ disembodied _____, otherworldly voice echoed through the dark halls.

14. When asked what was wrong, he shrugged _____ dismissively _____ and said nothing.

15. No one could penetrate their _____ disguise _____; they were masked, unknown and incognito.

The Latin prefix **de-**

Morphotextual Mastery: *Read the passage silently. Write a prefix on the line to complete the unfinished words. Circle or highlight all the words that begin with a prefix that means 'not' or 'opposite' (un-, non-, dis-, in-, im-, il-, ir-). Summarize, retelling main ideas to a partner. Read the passage aloud to develop fluency.*

Tips for Tomato Growers

Tomato plants do not grow quickly. They are slow to take root. They are slow to bear fruit. This plant is not a good choice for a gardener who is not patient. An _im_ patient gardener should plant radishes, because radishes develop more quickly than tomatoes. With tomatoes, one must be patient. After more than two months, the fully developed, mature plant will bear fruit—ripe, red, and sweet.

Tomatoes grow best in direct sunlight. (Indirect) light that is filtered by the leaves of a tree is not sufficiently intense. Under _in_ direct light, in deep shade, the fruit will become (imperfect.) It will be too small. It will not be sweet. Tomatoes need direct sunlight in order to become sweet and perfect.

Tomatoes need a constant and regular amount of water each day. An (inconstant,) _ir_ regular water supply is not good for the tomato. It is best to water these plants at the same time each day. It is advisable to water tomatoes in the morning or the evening. It is _in_ correct to water these plants in the blistering heat of the afternoon sun.

A tomato plant becomes heavy as it grows. The branches and the vines are too weak and frail to stand upright, so the whole plant sprawls all over the ground. There, on the soil, the tomato becomes a victim to insects, mold, and mice. Moldy tomatoes are _in_ edible and must be (discarded,) thrown away. The expert tomato gardener knows how to correct this problem. Experts insert an _in_ flexible wire frame around the tomato. The tomato branches curl around the frame. The vines cling to the frame. The _un_ bending frame supports the weight of the tomato. The plant stands upright—it does not sprawl—despite its weight.

Patient gardeners plants tomatoes in early spring. They plant tomatoes in direct sunlight. They water the plants regularly, at a constant time of day, in constant amounts. They support the plant with a framework made of (inflexible) wire. After almost three months, their patience is rewarded.

Reread this sentence: Experts insert an inflexible wire frame around the tomato. *What does the prefix* **in-** *indicate in the word* **insert**? *Circle one:* 'not, opposite'   OR ('in, inside')

Decide if the bold-type target word has been changed to a noun, adjective, verb, or adverb. Adverbs often end with the suffix -ly. Before beginning, study the lesson and example.

> Mother Teresa was *caring*. ▶▶ *Caring* is an **adjective** that describes Mother Teresa.
>
> Her heart was full of *care*. ▶▶ *Care* is a **noun** (person, place, thing, idea).
>
> She *caringly* fed the children. ▶▶ *Caringly* is an **adverb** that tells how she fed them.
>
> Mother Teresa *cared* for people. ▶▶ *Cared* is a **verb**; it states the action.

Example: Gloria was diabetic, so she had to watch her sugar intake. She had to be aware, or *conscious*, of the sweets she ate. ___adjective___

1. While watching television, Gloria half-*consciously* ate a dozen cookies. ___adverb___

2. Too much sugar rendered her *unconscious*. ___adjective___

3. Gloria was *unconscious* for a long time, lying in a vulnerable position. ___adjective___

4. For five hours she rested *unconsciously* on the carpet. ___adverb___

5. She finally regained *consciousness* in the hospital. ___noun___

6. At that point in time, Gloria made a *conscious* decision to avoid sweets. ___adjective___

7. She *consciously* avoided the candy aisle and the cookie jar. ___adverb___

8. It was harder to avoid her own *subconscious*. ___noun___

9. Images of sweets from television ads *subconsciously* bombarded her mind. ___adverb___

10. Nonetheless, Gloria was determined to never again eat so many sweets that she *unconsciously* fell into a diabetic coma. ___adverb___

The Latin prefix **trans**-; The Greek prefix **dia**-

 Part A: *Analogies. With a partner, finish each analogy with one of these words. Two words are decoys; do not use them.*

translator	transparent	transplant
transportation	transformation	transmission

1. **Window** is to _____transparent_____ as **mirror** is to **reflective**.

2. **Truck** is to _____transportation_____ as **oven** is to **food preparation**.

3. **Replace** is to _____transplant_____ as **notice** is to **observe**.

4. A _____translator_____ is to **communication** as a **doctor** is to **health**.

Part B: **Trans**- *means* across, through, *or* over. *Write* across, through, *or* over *on the line.*

1. To transport something is to ship it _____across (or over)_____ the land, the sea, or the air.

2. We can see _____through_____ transparent materials, like glass.

3. The sailboat sailed _____across_____ the Atlantic Ocean in the transatlantic race.

Part C: *Choose from the word bank to complete each sentence. Write the letter on the line.*

Word bank	Incomplete statement
A. diagonal	I found the _E_ of the engine on page sixteen.
B. diameter	_D_ marks are used to show the pronunciation of words.
C. dialogue	People in this part of the country speak an unusual _G_.
D. diacritical	Mayor Brown is _F_ opposed to city expansion.
E. diagram	The two friends carried on an interesting _C_.
F. diametrically	How do you measure the _B_ of that sphere?
G. dialect	Draw a _A_ line from one corner to the other.

Vocabulary Through Morphemes / Prefixes

Practice Page / 125

Vocabulary Through Morphemes / Teacher's Guide

The Latin prefix ex-

Choose the correct word to complete the sentence. Write the matching letter.

Word bank	Incomplete statement	Answer
A. exhibition	We inhale oxygen and we ____ carbon dioxide.	D
B. express	Explode is the opposite of ____.	N
C. exclude	Inclusion unites people but ____ divides people.	M
D. exhale	Does Japan ____ computer chips to America?	F
E. intrude	He made an ____ of himself when he danced on the table.	A
F. export	Excited people ____ themselves with gestures.	B
G. inhibit	When will the whale ____ from the water?	O
H. explosion	Mr. Mart's broken bone seemed to ____ from his arm.	P
I. extrovert	The student worried that everyone would ____ her.	C
J. exhalation	Her timidity will ____ her; she is too shy to sing in public.	G
K. evacuate	I am a shy introvert but my sociable brother is an ____.	I
L. exhibit	The engineer set off an ____ that destroyed the building.	H
M. exclusion	The bold young artist will ____ his paintings today.	L
N. implode	The baby's ___ is steady; he is breathing well.	J
O. emerge	In case of fire we must quickly ____ the building.	K
P. extrude	We do not want anyone to ____ into our personal life.	E

The Latin prefix **inter-** and **intra-**

Part A: *Decide if the target word (having **inter-** or **intra-**) implies between or within.*

	Phrase	Between	Within
Example:	a brief intermission after the third act of the play	✓	
1.	intercede to calm the hostile, angry neighbors	✓	
2.	distracted by a loud interruption	✓	
3.	interject an important comment	✓	
4.	staying alive through intravenous feeding		✓
5.	playing a lively game with lots of human interaction	✓	
6.	uncertain, unsure, experiencing intrapsychic conflict		✓

Part B: *Briefly define using **between** or **within the same**.*

	Phrase	Brief definition (using *between* or *within the same*)
Example:	intrastate waterway	a waterway within the same state
Example:	interplanetary wars	wars between planets
1.	an intramuscular disease	a disease within muscles
2.	an international spy	a spy from a different nation
3.	an intranet connection	a connection within some users of the Internet
4.	Internet access	a connection between all users of the Internet
5.	interstate highway	a highway that runs between states

The Latin prefix ad-

 Analogies: *With a partner, complete each analogy. Use words found in the word bank. One word is a decoy and should not be used.*

adhere	affirmation	ascend
adaptation	aspire	arrest

1. **Ladder** is to _____ascend_____ as **shovel** is to **excavate**.

2. **Quarreling** is to **disharmony** as _____adaptation_____ is to **survival**.

3. **Assistance** is to **injury** as _____affirmation_____ is to **discouragement**.

4. _____Arrest_____ is to **apprehend** as **slumber** is to **sleep**.

5. **Hope** is to _____aspire_____ as **proclaim** is to **announce**.

Morphotextual Mastery: *Read the passage silently. Write a prefix on the line to complete the unfinished words. Paraphrase the story, using synonyms for each boldface word. Summarize, retelling main ideas to a partner. Read the passage aloud to develop fluency..*

Chip In

Rita Williams and Rico Martinez are friends and business partners. They have been *collaborating* for years. When they first met, they were __co__ workers in the same company. They *collaborated* to manufacture electronics *components*. Soon they realized that they had an __un__ usual ability to *cooperate* together and to *communicate* with each other. Naturally, they decided to start their own business in the future.

Years later, Rita and Rico *cofounded* "Chip In," an electronics firm that promised to give a sizeable percentage of its profits to charity (at least 20 percent). The two were _co_ -owners of the new company. They asked several *colleagues* from their former job to join them at Chip In. Soon hundreds of people were working with them.

To *cooperatively* run the company, Rita and Rico divided the responsibilities. It was Rita's job to *coordinate* the tasks so that all manufacturing departments worked in *concert*. Rita had an aptitude for organization, *coordination*, and administration. It was Rico's job to *communicate* with the employees and the public. Rico was a great *conversationalist*. He could form *connections* with people quickly and easily. He could get people to _co_ operate.

Chip In was very successful. By the third year, company earnings *exceeded* expectations. Rita and Rico had to set up a special *committee* to decide how to distribute the profits to the charities. Hopeless people in neighboring *communities* were _ex_ ceedingly glad to get help.

Rita and Rico are now semiretired, but they *continue* to work together occasionally. They are _co_ *authors* of the book *Plenty*. Their book explains how to create a *community-centered business*. The two colleagues *correspond* with each other frequently. They have never lost their unusual aptitude for *communication*.

The Greek prefix mon- (spelled mono-, mona-)

Finish each sentence. Use words with the prefix **mon-** *(***mono-**, **mona-***)*. *For help, refer to the opposite page.*

1. Writing my name 100 times was boring, very _____ monotonous _____.

2. Let's ride the _____ monorail _____ up the mountain.

3. My teacher speaks five languages; she is not _____ monolingual _____.

4. The belief that there is only one god is called _____ monotheism _____.

5. I have a _____ monogram _____ of my name sewn into my sweatshirt.

6. The _____ monarch _____ is the king of the butterflies.

7. I would like to be in the choir, but my singing voice is a _____ monotone _____.

8. A single large block of stone is called a _____ monolith _____.

9. We plan to study scriptures at the _____ monastery _____.

10. He looked through his _____ monocle _____ at the menu.

11. A _____ monoplane _____ is an airplane with only one pair of wings.

12. A _____ monopoly _____ happens when one company with no competition sells a product.

BONUS ACTIVITY **Multisensory, see page 165**

Morphotextual Mastery: *Working with a partner, complete the passage. Use words from the bank. Use one word twice. Read the passage aloud to develop fluency.*

union	united	likelihood	document	leadership
victorious	expel	monarchy	exceedingly	exited

Unity

In 1775, King George of England ruled the thirteen colonies in America. However, the American colonists did not appreciate his style of ___leadership___. They did not appreciate paying ever-increasing taxes. They wanted to form a new government—a democracy or a republic or maybe a federation—anything but a ___monarchy___.

The American colonists decided to ___expel___ all the British Redcoats—boot out all the king's horses and all the king's men. Thus, the thirteen colonies ___united___ into one collective organization, one union. Able-bodied citizens formed the first American army. It was a barefoot army—a ragtag army—a horseless army. What was the ___likelihood___ that this poorly equipped army would outfight the British Redcoats? But they did! They were ___victorious___! King George was ___exceedingly___ surprised when the ragged American army won the war. His Redcoats ___exited___ America and returned to England. After the war, the thirteen colonies stayed in the union. The United States of America emerged.

After the war, the Constitution was written. It was written by a committee—a group united for one goal. The Preamble to the Constitution states:

> We the people of the United States, in order to form a more perfect ___union___, establish justice, insure domestic tranquility, provide for the common defense, promote the general welfare, and secure the blessings of liberty to ourselves and our posterity, do ordain and establish this Constitution for the United States of America.

This ___document___ forms the backbone of American government. It is the law of the land, so to speak. One nation, under one document, ___united___.

Write a simple definition for each word. Use the words **one** *or* **two**, *as shown in the examples.*

		Definition using *one* or *two*
Example:	bicycle	two cycles or two wheels
Example:	monorail	one rail
Example:	digraph	two letters representing one sound, as in *sh, ch, th*
1.	bilingual	
2.	binoculars	(Answers will vary.)
3.	bipolar	
4.	bipartisan	
5.	biweekly	
6.	uniforms	
7.	bimonthly	
8.	duet	
9.	biennial	
10.	dioxide	
11.	bifocals	
12.	monosyllabic	
13.	diatomic	
14.	dichromatic	
15.	unison	
16.	duplex	

The Latin/Greek prefix **tri-**

Part A: *Write the word that matches the definition. Choose words from the word bank. Refer to the opposite page for help.*

triplets	tricycle	triangle	triathlon
triceratops	triceps	trilobite	trilogy
trinity	trident	triple	tripod

Example: a group of three   ____triple____

1. having three wheels   ____tricycle____

2. a muscle with three ends   ____triceps____

3. three closely related members   ____trinity____

4. having three angles   ____triangle____

5. extinct animal that had three horns near its eyes   ____triceratops____

6. three combined stories   ____trilogy____

7. extinct marine creature that had three lobes   ____trilobite____

8. three athletic events in one   ____triathlon____

9. a support having three legs   ____tripod____

10. three babies born from the same egg   ____triplets____

11. a three-pronged fork used to spear fish   ____trident____

 Part B: *Let's tell some riddles!*

1. What do you call a fast tricycle? (a tot rod)

2. What's the difference between a triathlete and a locomotive engineer?
    (One trains to run; the other runs the train.)

3. What did the judge say to the rowdy milk bottles? ("Order in the quart!")

The Latin prefix **multi-**; The Greek prefix **poly-**

*Read each sentence. Underline or highlight each numeric prefix. Write the exact number the prefix denotes above the word. Write > **1** to indicate '2 or more' (before beginning, study the examples).*

Example: We speak French, Spanish, English, and Italian; we are <u>multi</u>lingual. `>1`

Example: A symphony is <u>poly</u>phonic—we can hear many sounds at the same time. `>1`

Example: Monks live alone, without a wife or family, in a <u>mona</u>stery. `1`

1. Even a <u>multi</u>millionaire must sleep and eat and use the facilities. `>1`

2. A person who speaks several languages is <u>multi</u>lingual, also known as a <u>poly</u>glot. `>1` `>1`

3. A clown in a <u>multi</u>colored gown rode a <u>uni</u>cycle in the parade. `>1` `1`

4. In many cultures <u>poly</u>gamy—having <u>multi</u>ple spouses at the same time—is illegal. `>1` `>1`

5. At the <u>Poly</u>tech, we study the <u>multi</u>dimensional aspects of science, math, and music. `>1` `>1`

6. What is <u>mono</u>theism, and which religions practice <u>mono</u>theistic worship? `1` `1`

7. We saw three different movies this month at the <u>multi</u>plex. `>1`

8. This cooking oil is <u>poly</u>unsaturated. `>1`

9. A <u>multi</u>tude of employees work in that <u>multi</u>story office building. `>1` `>1`

10. A <u>uni</u>corn is a mythical animal with one horn (in Latin, *corn* means 'horn'). `1`

11. St. Nick is <u>multi</u>generational and <u>multi</u>cultural; many people know of him. `>1` `>1`

12. The choir sang the <u>uni</u>versally known song "Amazing Grace" in perfect <u>uni</u>son. `1` `1`

13. We <u>multi</u>task, painting our nails as we listen to the first book in the <u>tri</u>logy. `>1` `3`

Greek and Latin numeric prefixes

Part A: *Read each sentence. Highlight each numeric prefix. Write the exact number the prefix denotes above the word. Write* **> 1** *to indicate '2 or more' or write* **half**. *Before beginning, study the example.*

Example: Looking through a pair of <u>bi</u>noculars, I could see the <u>semi</u>trailer enter the tunnel.
(2) ... (half)

1. Carbon <u>mon</u>oxide and carbon <u>di</u>oxide emissions are harmful to the environment.
(1) ... (2)

2. She gave birth to <u>tri</u>plets; her cat birthed <u>quadr</u>uplets and her rabbit bore <u>quint</u>uplets.
(3) ... (4) ... (5)

3. Both a <u>milli</u>pede and a <u>centi</u>pede are <u>poly</u>pods; they have numerous feet.
(1,000) ... (100) ... (>1)

4. A <u>poly</u>graph machine measures changes in heartbeat, blood pressure, and respiration.
(>1)

5. He participated in the <u>bi</u>athlon, she joined the <u>tri</u>athlon, and I entered the <u>deca</u>thlon.
(2) ... (3) ... (10)

6. Carefully, the jeweler placed a <u>multi</u>faceted <u>semi</u>precious stone into tiny golden brackets.
(>1) ... (half)

7. If you live an entire <u>cent</u>ury, how old are you? How long is a <u>millenn</u>ium?
(100) ... (1,000)

8. In October, an <u>octo</u>pus played an <u>octa</u>ve on the piano. Do-re-mi-fa-so-la-ti-do!
(8) ... (8) ... (8)

Part B: *Morphotextual Mastery. Write a number or word on each line. For help, look for context clues and morpheme clues and look at prior pages. Paraphrase the passage to a partner. Read it aloud to develop fluency.*

Naming the Months: Exploring Word Origins

Why does October begin with the prefix **oct-** meaning ____eight____ when it is actually the tenth month of the year? This is because in the old Roman calendar, March was the first month of the year, named after *Mars*, the Roman war god. September, with **septem** meaning ____seven____, was the seventh month. The eighth month was ____October____. Later, the Romans changed their calendar to make January the ____first____ month of the year, named for *Janus*, the Roman god of beginnings. Every month moved back two, so March went from being first to being third. The old fifth month (*Quintilis*) was renamed July, in honor of Julius Caesar. The old sixth month (*Sextilis*) was changed to ____August____, in honor of Caesar Augustus. We still use this Julian calendar today. In Roman numerals, the year 2011 is written as MMXI. The year 2105 will be written as MMCV (C is for ____one hundred____).
(100)

BONUS ACTIVITY   Multisensory, see pages 167 and 169

Highlight or underline the word that begins with **pre-** *in each sentence. Write the word on the line, separating the prefix from the rest of the word as shown in the example. Read each math statement aloud.*

	Word beginning with *pre-*
Example: Health insurance can no longer be withheld if you have a <u>preexisting</u> condition.	pre- + existing
1. His meteorological <u>predictions</u> did not occur.	pre- + dictions
2. "Around the tree" is a <u>prepositional</u> phrase.	pre- + positional
3. Fix the <u>prefix</u> in place before the base or root.	pre- + fix
4. Before she read the book, she <u>previewed</u> it carefully.	pre- + viewed
5. We <u>preheated</u> the oven before we baked the pie.	pre- + heated
6. Sadly, the accused felt <u>prejudged</u> before the trial began.	pre- + judged
7. Hikers found <u>prehistoric</u> fossils in the cave.	pre- + historic
8. Twelve happy <u>preschoolers</u> sang a little tune.	pre- + schoolers
9. When does the <u>preseason</u> football game begin?	pre- + season
10. Expecting a baby, she is taking <u>prenatal</u> vitamins.	pre- + natal
11. As a <u>precautionary</u> measure, we packed a first aid kit.	pre- + cautionary
12. Dr. Jones wrote a <u>prescription</u> for penicillin.	pre- + scription

The Latin prefix post-

Part A: *Choose the correct word to complete the sentence. Write the matching letter in the last column.*

Word bank	Incomplete statement	Answer
A. postpone	The attorneys held a _____ meeting before the judge appeared.	F
B. preparations	After undergoing hypnosis, she fell into a _____ trance.	I
C. postwar	"May we _____ to share your table?" begged Alicia and Tara.	D
D. presume	Dr. Boyd ran several _____ blood tests to rule out diabetes.	H
E. posterity	Exit the building through the _____ door.	J
F. pretrial	A _____ is positioned before an object, as in "on the hat."	K
G. prejudice	_____ for the dance began right after school.	B
H. preliminary	Due to the rain, we must _____ the football game.	A
I. posthypnotic	We planted trees for _____, for our grandchildren to enjoy.	E
J. posterior	A judge must be free of all _____ and bias.	G
K. preposition	After the Civil War, our country endured _____ confusion.	C

(F. pretrial is circled in the word bank.)

Part B: *Draw a picture of a building, a vehicle, or something else. Label the interior, exterior, posterior, and anterior (for help, review the limo story on the opposite page). In the picture, draw someone with an ulterior motive. Write a sentence to explain your scene. Show it to a partner.*

(Answers will vary.)

Sentence: _____

The Latin prefixes **mal-** and **bene-**

Highlight words having a positive connotation in one color. Use a different color for words that carry a negative shade of meaning. Leave neutral words blank.

(Answers will vary. No key.)

benefit	replenish	confusion	malign
malnourished	accompany	malice	companion
benign	benediction	cooperation	distressed
unify	malevolent	benevolence	exterminate
restore	universe	interracially	beneficial
unity	community	revival	malady
maltreatment	destructive	benefactor	malformed

Write the complete word. Drop the letters that are in parentheses.

Example:	mis- + spell + -ing	misspelling
1.	mis- + trust + -ed	mistrusted
2.	un- + mis- + tak(e) + -able	unmistakable
3.	mis- + guid(e) + -ed + -ly	misguidedly
4.	mis- + pro- + nounc(e) + -ed	mispronounced
5.	mis- + shap(e) + -en	misshapen
6.	mis- + calculat(e) + -ed	miscalculated
7.	mis- + inter- + pret + -ation	misinterpretation
8.	mis- + dia- + gno + -sis	misdiagnosis
9.	mis- + place + -ment	misplacement
10.	mis- + direct + -ed	misdirected
11.	mis- + ally (*y* changes to *i*) + -ance	misalliance
12.	mal- + pract + -ice	malpractice
13.	mal- + odor + -ous	malodorous
14.	bene- + fit + -ed	benefited
15.	bene- + dict + -ion	benediction
16.	bene- + fic + -ial	beneficial

The Latin prefix **pro-**

Challenge! *Choose a word from the bank to complete each sentence according to the grammatical function (verb, noun, adjective, adverb). Then read the entire page. It tells a story.*

All the words in the bank contain *gress* (a Latin root meaning 'to step').

Congress	transgression	progressing	congressional	egress
regress	aggression	progressively	progressive	progress

		Meaning	Word (answer)
Example:	Mia was (verb)	step forward	progressing
Example:	She was making (noun) in her political science classes.	step forward	progress
1.	Mia's professor knew that Mia was positive and (adjective).	step forward	progressive
2.	He was sure that she would eventually serve with the (proper noun) of the United States.	step with	Congress
3.	To that end, he arranged for Mia to work as a (adjective) aide.	step with	congressional
4.	He warned Mia not to be too pushy—not to show (noun).	forceful step	aggression
5.	He warned her that an illegal (noun) would destroy her career.	step across	transgression
6.	Unwilling to (verb), Mia was careful to be polite and honest.	step backward	regress
7.	She had no wish to (verb) through the nearest political exit.	step out	egress
8.	Working (adverb), Mia was making her way to Capitol Hill.	step forward	progressively

Choose a word from the word bank to complete each sentence. One word is a decoy.

encampment	empowered	enable	enliven
entrap	(enact)	envenom	environment
engrossing	engagement	ennoble	employees
enlighten	ensnared	embellished	enlarge

Example: The sixth grade class will ___ a play. — **enact**

1. Investigator Stanwick attempted to ___ the thief. — **entrap**

2. We need to ___ the kitchen. — **enlarge**

3. Loud music will ___ this dull party. — **enliven**

4. Can great books ___ us? — **enlighten or ennoble**

5. One ugly spider ___ a poor little fly. — **ensnared**

6. Tomorrow's ___ is in our hands today. — **environment**

7. Molly was reading a totally ___ novel. — **engrossing**

8. His troops set up an ___ on the hilltop. — **encampment**

9. Kind and gracious acts ___ every heart. — **ennoble**

10. We are ___ of the library. — **employees**

11. ___ by new hope, he began to dig faster. — **empowered**

12. Beth dressed carefully for an important ___. — **engagement**

13. Red bows and white lights ___ our lovely tree. — **embellished**

14. These tools will ___ us to build a fort. — **enable**

The Latin prefix be-

Choose words from the word bank to match the meaning.

because	bemoan	betray	beside	bedazzled
belie	belittle	behold	between	believe
bewildered	(befriend)	beholden	become	bejeweled
beleaguered	beyond	behind		

Meaning	Term
Example: to be a friend to	befriend
1. to deceive, sell out	betray
2. to the rear or the hind end	behind
3. to the side	beside
4. a midpoint in position or time	between
5. to be farther away from	beyond
6. to be the cause of	because
7. to come into being	become
8. completely covered in jewels	bejeweled
9. completely dazzled	bedazzled
10. completely lost, confused	bewildered
11. completely overwhelmed (as by leagues of enemies)	beleaguered
12. to make a lie of	belie
13. to trust, accept as true	believe
14. to moan, as with regret, sadness, fear, or pain	bemoan
15. to see, to hold in your sight	behold
16. to be held, as a debt; to repay	beholden
17. to make little of, to put down	belittle

Summative Assessment

Morphotextual Mastery: *Read the passage silently. Write a prefix on the line to complete the unfinished words. With a partner, paraphrase the story, using synonyms for each boldface word. Read the passage aloud to develop fluency.*

Majestic Mountain is a ***scenic*** but dangerous hiking area. ***Inexperienced*** climbers frequently fall as they ascend or descend the mountain, __en__ dangering their lives. One __mis__ step can be deadly. When ***mishaps*** occur, the rescue team is called.

Stormcloud is the __un__ official leader of the voluntary search and rescue squad. Most of the volunteers have full-time jobs elsewhere. They work for Stormcloud not to ***enrich*** themselves but to ***beneficially employ*** their natural mountaineering skills. Stormcloud ***deploys*** old Kitty Mason to the scene whenever there is an injury because Kitty is a doctor.

Occasionally, Kitty can ***foretell*** or __pre__ dict when an accident will happen; she says she can feel it in her bones. On this particular day, Kitty had a ***premonition*** that the phone would ring, and indeed it did. "I need you immediately!" Stormcloud stated urgently. Kitty ***denounced*** his bad timing, ***bemoaning*** that her soup was nearly ready. But she grabbed her portable medical kit. ***Presently***, she was seated beside Stormcloud in a helicopter.

On an ***inaccessible*** ledge, an adolescent was unconscious. He had fallen twenty feet because he had __mis__ takenly stepped onto slippery, stony rubble. His hysterical father was nearly beside himself with anxiety. With ***forethought***, Kitty had packed a ***deflated*** splint cushion in her kit. She assigned a task to the panicking father: "You must inflate this cushion," she said. This task helped calm the __mal__ functioning parent. Meanwhile, Kitty inspected the injured youth. His leg looked __un__ natural. Kitty took the now fully inflated splint and wrapped it around the broken leg, strapping it in place. The cushion ***immobilized*** the leg so the fracture could not get any worse. It enabled them to transfer the boy to a stretcher.

The helicopter __trans__ ported them to the hospital. Two porters carried the stretcher into the emergency room. "Thank you, ma'am!" the father told Kitty. "I'm ***beholden*** to you!"

"You're most welcome!" Kitty told the ***becalmed*** father. She encouraged him to drink some water because he looked __de__ hydrated. Soon Kitty was back at home, __re__ heating her cold soup. She hoped there would be no more injuries for the ***foreseeable*** future.

Assessment continued on page 161.

Part A: *Choose prefixes from the word bank to match the meaning.*

re-	(sub-)	bi-, di-, du-	ex-, e-	anti-, contra-	pro-
intra-	co-, com-	mono-, uni-	trans-	post-	multi-, poly-
pre-	tri-	mal-	bene-	mis-	inter-

Example: under, less important   _____sub-_____

1. across, through   _____trans-_____

2. before   _____pre-_____

3. three   _____tri-_____

4. within the same   _____intra-_____

5. good, well   _____bene-_____

6. bad, evil   _____mal-_____

7. forward, forth, toward   _____pro-_____

8. two   _____bi-, di-, du-_____

9. after   _____post-_____

10. one, single   _____mono-, uni-_____

11. with, together   _____co-, com- (col, cor-)_____

12. against   _____anti-, contra-_____

13. wrong, incorrect   _____mis-_____

14. back, again   _____re-_____

15. many, much, several   _____multi-, poly-_____

16. out   _____ex-, e-_____

17. between, among   _____inter-_____

Part B: *Cross out the prefixes that usually have a **negative** meaning.*

~~anti-~~   ~~dis-~~   trans-   pro-   ~~de-~~   ~~il-~~   co-

~~non-~~   ~~contra-~~   ~~un-~~   ~~in-~~   com-   ~~mal-~~   bene-

The Greek forms **astro** and **bio**

Part A: *Choose the correct word to match the definition. Write the word.*

astronomer	astronomy	astrologist
astronaut	asterisk	asteroids
aster	~~astronavigation~~	

Example: the process of navigating by the stars — astronavigation

1. the study of stars, galaxies, the heavens — astronomy

2. a star-shaped flower — aster

3. small bodies that revolve around the sun — asteroids

4. one who studies the heavens to see the future — astrologist

5. one who studies the galaxies, stars, heavens — astronomer

6. star-shaped mark used to note a reference in text — asterisk

7. one who goes on a voyage to the heavens — astronaut

Part B: *Highlight the correct word.*

1. (Biology, Biomass) is the study of life and living organisms.

2. A (biopsy, biography) is the story of a person's life.

3. A (biologician, biologist) studies life and living organisms.

4. The earth is a (biodegradable, biosphere)—a sphere that supports and sustains life.

5. A bioluminescent animal gives off its own (life, light).

6. Something that is (biodegradable, bionic) can be broken down by small living organisms.

7. Folks living in Siberia must endure a cold and punishing (biome, biography).

Part A: *Choose from the words in the word bank to match the given meaning.*

geodes	geothermal	geologist
geologic	geopolitical	geography
geophysical		

Example: related to the study of the earth   geologic

1. related to the physics of the earth   geophysical

2. the study of the lands and peoples of earth   geography

3. one who studies the earth, soil, ground   geologist

4. related to heat generated inside the earth   geothermal

5. related to the people and politics of the earth   geopolitical

6. hollow, spherical rocks lined with crystals   geodes

Part B: *Does the definition match the word? Mark **Yes** or **No**.*

	Definition	Word	Yes?	No?
1.	used to keep liquids hot (or cold)	thermos	✓	
2.	related to ice; producing or creating ice	thermal		✓
3.	related to a process that absorbs heat in	endothermic	✓	
4.	related to a process that releases heat out	exothermic	✓	
5.	related to heat inside the human body	geothermic		✓
6.	a tool used to measure temperature	thermometer	✓	
7.	a device used to set the temperature	hypothermia		✓
8.	electricity generated by heat	thermoelectricity	✓	

Write the roots and affixes that make up the word. Some words have more than one root. They behave like compound words. Look back in prior pages to review Greek roots.

Example:	biographical	bio- + graph + -ic + -al
Example:	autobiography	auto- + bio- + graph + -y
1.	autodestruct	auto- + destruct (or auto- + de- + struct)
2.	automotive	auto- + motive (or auto- + mot + -ive)
3.	automatic	auto- + matic (or auto- + mat + -ic)
4.	autograph	auto- + graph
5.	thermonuclear	thermo- + nuclear (or thermo- + nucle + -ar)
6.	thermoelectric	thermo- + electric (or thermo- + electr + -ic)
7.	geothermal	geo- + thermal (or geo- + therm + -al)
8.	astrology	astro- + -ology
9.	geophysical	geo- + physical (or geo- + phys + -ic + -al)
10.	biodegradable	bio- + degrade + -able (or bio- + de- + grade + -able)
11.	biochemical	bio- + chemical (or bio- + chem + -ic + -al)
12.	autocratic	auto- + cratic (or auto- + crat + -ic)
13.	automobile	auto- + mobile (or auto- + mob + -ile)
14.	astrobiology	astro- + biology (or astro- + bio + -ology)

BONUS ACTIVITY Multisensory, see page 225

Part A: *Morphotextual Mastery: Read the passage silently. Working with a partner, paraphrase the story, using synonyms for each bold-type word. Read the passage aloud to develop fluency.*

Inspector Swift

Inspector Swift worked in the **homicide** department in Seattle, Washington. It was his job to determine whether death had occurred through natural causes, through **homicide**, or through suicide. It was a grisly job, and often frustrating, but Swift was one of the best.

One particular murder occurred in a very **homogenous** neighborhood that surrounded a lake. In this area, every family was similar, having two well-educated parents, one or two children, a few pets, a nanny, and several vehicles. Every family in this **homogenous** neighborhood had a **substantial income** as well.

A hydrologist had been killed while taking water samples from the lake. In the lake, the scientist had discovered a **semi-deadly** toxin—a poison. **Hydrologists** see themselves as protectors of the **hydrosphere**. The scientist had been planning to publish his findings in the next issue of the *Journal of Hydrology* and to alert the **environmental officials**.

To prevent the hydrologist from reporting his discovery, two lakeside homeowners **collaborated** in his murder. Inspector Swift charged the homeowners with murder by poison. He identified the motive as **financial** interests. Swift argued that this **homicide** had occurred as the homeowners' **attempt** to maintain the value of their real estate.

Now the earth has lost one fine **hydrologist**. A few men from a **homogenous** neighborhood are behind bars, and Inspector Swift has moved on to his next **homicide** investigation.

Part B: *Write the meaning of each word. Look for morpheme clues and reread the passage for context clues.*

1. homicide _____ Answers will vary. _____

2. homogenous _____

3. hydrologist _____

4. hydrosphere _____

5. collaborated _____

6. substantial income _____

The Greek forms **phon/phone** *and* **scop/scope**

 Part A: *Reorder the scrambled morphemes. Write the whole word. Talk about the word's meaning.*

Example:	phon	caco	y			cacophony (bad, displeasing sounds)
1.	ic	poly	phon			polyphonic
2.	y	phon	sym			symphony
3.	phone	s	tele			telephones
4.	s	phone	micro			microphones
5.	ic	s	phon			phonics
6.	ize	hydro	gen			hydrogenize
7.	bio	auto	ic	graph	al	autobiographical
8.	graph	ic	geo	al		geographical
9.	meter	s	thermo			thermometers
10.	log	ic	astro	al		astrological

Part B: *Choose the correct word from the word bank to complete the sentence. Write the word.*

hydroscope	microscope	stethoscope	(kaleidoscope)
telescope	chronoscope	periscope	

Example: Shake the _____kaleidoscope_____ and look inside at colorful, geometric shapes.

1. Dr. Diaz listens to my heart with a _____stethoscope_____.

2. A _____chronoscope_____ measures or observes the passage of time.

3. Astrologists look at distant stars with a _____telescope_____.

4. A _____hydroscope_____ is used to measure the depth of the water.

5. Tiny particles may be magnified with a _____microscope_____.

6. Submarine captains can view the surrounding area with a _____periscope_____.

Part A: *Write the antonym (opposite meaning) for each one. Use* **micro** *or* **macro**.

Term	Antonym
Example: microscopic	macroscopic
1. macroclimate	microclimate
2. microcosm	macrocosm
3. microphysics	macrophysics
4. macroeconomics	microeconomics
5. micronucleus	macronucleus

Part B: *Finish each sentence.*

Example: A microscope is an instrument used to magnify very ____small____ objects.

1. Macroscopic objects are ____large____ enough to be seen clearly with the unaided human eye.

2. Microscopic objects are too ____small (or tiny)____ to be seen clearly with the unaided human eye.

3. A microphysicist studies very ____small (or tiny)____ molecules, atoms, and nuclear systems.

4. A microclimate has weather that occurs only in a very ____small____ geographic area.

5. Surgeons perform microsurgery on ____small (or tiny)____ nerve endings.

6. Study macroeconomics to note ____large____ changes in income across the nation.

7. A ____microphone (or megaphone)____ is used by a sports announcer to amplify or enlarge small sounds.

8. Microorganisms are very ____small (or tiny)____ ____organisms____ , such as bacteria.

The Greek forms **graph/gram** and **photo**

Part A: *Write the correct term on the line. Use words found in the word bank. One word is a decoy.*

homograph	photograph	calligraphy
phonograph	telegram	monogram
⟨geography⟩		

Example: writings about the earth, peoples, maps   geography

1. written in one, combined in one   monogram

2. written the same   homograph

3. written with elegance and style   calligraphy

4. written with sound   phonograph

5. written from a distance   telegram

Part B: *How many recognizable morphemes (prefixes, roots or base words, suffixes) are in each word? Write the number.*

Example: photomicroscopes   4   (photo + micro + scope + s)

Example: photography   3

1. photographer   3

2. photographers   4

3. telephoto   2

4. photographic   3

5. photobiotic   3

The Greek forms **tele** and **meter**

Part A: *Add more related words to each column.*

Answers may vary.

forms of *telescope*	words containing *tele*	words containing *scope*
telescopes	telephone	microscope
telescoping	telegraph	stethoscope
telescopic	telephoto lens	telescope
	telegram	kaleidoscope

Part B: *Finish each sentence. Look for clues in the sentences. Look back at prior pages for help.*

1. A _____ thermometer _____ is used to measure the temperature.

2. Very _____ small (or tiny) _____ objects are measured with a micrometer.

3. Time is _____ measured _____ with a chronometer, a watch, or a clock.

4. Chronometry is the science of measuring _____ time _____.

5. Changes in air pressure are _____ measured _____ with a barometer.

6. Barometry is the science of _____ measuring _____ air _____ pressure _____.

7. Radiometry is the _____ study _____ of _____ measuring _____ radiation.

8. A radiometer measures _____ radiation _____, or radiant energy.

Part A: *Pronouncing Greek words. When an English word flows from Greek, the final e is often pronounced, as in* **psychē.** *This is not a rule; it is a tendency.*

Read the words. Circle the words that end with a long **ē** sound, and mark the **e** with a line. If the word ends with a silent **e**, draw a slash through the final **e**. First, study the examples.

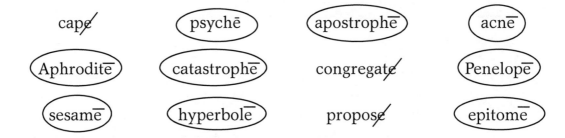

cap̸e   (psychē)   (apostrophē)   (acnē)

(Aphroditē)   (catastrophē)   congregat̸e   (Penelopē)

(sesamē)   (hyperbolē)   propos̸e   (epitomē)

 Part B: *Morphotextual Mastery: Read the story. With a partner, define the bold-type words. Examine context and morphemes for clues. Then, read the story aloud.*

Greek Mythology—Aphrodite, Psyche, and Eros

The ancient Greeks created stories about gods and mortals to explain human *psychology*. In Greek mythology, Aphrodite was the goddess of love. She was exceedingly beautiful and she knew it. Aphrodite was vain and prideful—*pathetically* absorbed in her own reflection.

One day, a lovely babe named Psyche was born. Psyche was the daughter of a mortal king. As the years passed, Psyche developed into an astoundingly beautiful princess. Aphrodite became increasingly jealous of Psyche's beauty. In her *pathological* jealousy, she decided to punish the innocent princess.

Aphrodite's son, Eros, was the god of love. When he shot his invisible arrows at humans, they instantly fell in love with the first person they saw. Aphrodite told her son to make Psyche fall for an old man with rotting teeth. Eros argued with his *psychotic* mother, urging her to see a *psychotherapist*, but she would not. Finally, he agreed to do as she asked.

Standing invisible, an arrow in his hand, Eros watched Psyche. He felt *compassion* because he knew she would be miserable with the old man. Sadly he rubbed his chin, accidentally scratching himself with his own arrow. In that instant, Eros fell *passionately* and wholeheartedly in love with Psyche.

What does Aphrodite do? How does Eros fight for Psyche? Find out for yourself. Different variations of this myth are stored on the World Wide Web.

BONUS ACTIVITY | Multisensory, see page 227

Part A: *Write the term that fits the definition. Choose from the words in the word bank. One word is a decoy.*

pantheon	panorama	pantomime
pantheism	panacea	pandemonium

1. the belief that gods are living in all of nature _____pantheism_____

2. to act out a message using your whole body _____pantomime_____

3. temple dedicated to all Roman gods _____pantheon_____

4. a universal cure for all illnesses _____panacea_____

5. a view of the whole area, everything all around _____panorama_____

Part B: *Finish each sentence. Refer to the opposite page for help.*

1. People visit a _____zoo_____ to see exotic animals from distant lands.

2. Zoology is the study of _____animals_____, their habitats, and their behaviors.

3. One who studies animals is known as a _____zoologist_____.

4. One who is zoophobic has an abnormal fear of _____animals_____.

5. Zoogeography is the study of the _____lands_____ where specific _____animals_____ live.

6. A poison that originates within an _____animal_____ is a zootoxin.

Part A: *Analogies. Working with a partner, finish each analogy. Highlight the correct answer, found in parentheses.*

- *Continuous* is to (**chronic,** *sporadic*) as *unexpected* is to *sudden*.
- *Swimming* is to (*chronicle,* **synchronized**) as *skating* is to *figure*.
- *Chronicle* is to (**news,** *recipes*) as *dictionary* is to *definitions*.

Part B: *Highlight the part of the word (morpheme) that matches the meaning in the first column. The first two are done for you.*

Example:	study of	This book tells the chron(ology) of techn(ology).
Example:	having, filled with	Eyeballs are aque(ous) in the center.
1.	measuring device	Use a chrono(meter) to keep track of the passage of time.
2.	animal	She is a member of the (zoo)logical society.
3.	all, whole	Some people think laughter is a (pan)acea for all illnesses.
4.	time	He has a persistent, recurring, (chron)ic cough.
5.	life	An aquarium is a (bio)sphere for fish.
6.	water	Water is composed of (hydro)gen and oxygen.
7.	water	She plans to become a (hydro)logist.
8.	time	Let's put all these birth dates in (chrono)logical order.

The Greek form phobia

Part A: *Write the term that matches the meaning. Use words from the bank. One is a decoy.*

photophobia	xenophobia	agoraphobia
claustrophobia	Francophobe	acrophobia
arachnophobia	zoophobia	hydrophobia

	Meaning	Type of illness
1.	fear of spiders	arachnophobia
2.	fear of wide-open spaces	agoraphobia
3.	fear of water (also another name for rabies)	hydrophobia
4.	fear of animals	zoophobia
5.	fear of heights	acrophobia
6.	fear of small, closed-in spaces	claustrophobia
7.	pain and distress caused by bright lights	photophobia
8.	a feeling of intense dislike for foreigners	xenophobia

Part B: *Finish each sentence. Find clues in the context and inside the words themselves. Also, refer to the opposite page for help.*

1. One who suffers from photophobia avoids bright _____lights_____.

2. An Anglophobic person _____fears_____ or _____dislikes_____ the English.

3. If you are a _____Francophobe_____, you would not want to visit Paris.

4. If you overcome your _____acrophobia_____, you could become an acrobat.

5. Little Miss Muffet may have been _____arachnophobic_____ because she feared spiders.

Assessment: Greek Combining Forms (Roots)

Write the root that matches the meaning. Roots are listed below. The words in parentheses are clues; do not write them.

scope (telescope)	astro, astr (astronaut)	graph, gram (biography)
chron (chronological)	cide (suicide)	zoo, zo (zoologist)
meter, metr (barometer)	phon, phone (telephone)	phobia (claustrophobia)
hydr, hydro (hydrogen)	micro (microscope)	auto, aut (automatic)
psych, psyche (psychology)	geo (geology)	tele (telescope)
hom, homo (homogenous)	therm (thermostat)	pan (pantheism)
path, pass (pathetic)	photo (photon)	bio (biology)

	Meaning	Greek root or combining form
Example:	water	hydr, hydro
1.	mind, mental	psych, psyche
2.	sound, speech, voice	phon, phone
3.	to see, a device for viewing	scope
4.	distant, far	tele
5.	to measure; a measuring device	meter, metr
6.	to kill (often used as a suffix)	cide
7.	self	auto, aut
8.	heat, warm, energy	therm
9.	earth, rocks, land	geo
10.	very small	micro
11.	time	chron
12.	to write, written	graph, gram
13.	suffering, disease	path, pass
14.	all, whole	pan
15.	fear or intense dislike, an illness	phobia
16.	stars, heavens, cosmos	astro, astr
17.	same, similar (or man, in some cases)	hom, homo
18.	animal	zoo, zo
19.	life, living organism	bio
20.	light	photo

The Latin roots **aqua** and **terr/terra**

Part A: *Working with a partner, finish each analogy. Highlight the correct answer, found in parentheses.*

- *Igloo* is to *ice* as *aquarium* is to *(water, glass).*
- *Splendiferous* is to *splendid* as *aqueous* is to *(ugly, watery).*
- *Astronaut* is to *the heavens* as *aquanaut* is to *(the oceans, the aquariums).*

Part B: *Highlight or circle the morpheme that matches the meaning in the first column.*

	Example:	water	Her favorite color is aquamarine.
1.		study of	He bought a book about paleontology.
2.		time	He has a persistent, recurring, chronic cough.
3.		measuring device	Use a metronome to maintain a measured rhythm.
4.		animal	She is a member of the zoological society.
5.		all, whole	Is aspirin is a panacea for all illnesses?
6.		water	Sam enjoys aquatic sports, such as swimming and diving.
7.		having, filled with	Eyeballs are aqueous in the center.
8.		water	An aquarium is an artificial home for fish.
9.		water	Romans irrigated their lands with aqueducts.
10.		time	Let put all these birth dates in chronological order.

Part C: *Finish the following sentence.*

The words *aquarium, gymnasium, auditorium, planetarium, solarium, stadium,* and *sanitarium* all have the same _____suffix_____, which is ____-ium____, which seems to make the word a _____noun_____. All these words are _____places_____.

The Latin roots **port** and **rupt**

Part A: *Break each word into its prefix, root, and suffixes. Write them in the correct column.*

	Word	Prefix	Root	Suffix	Suffix
Example:	interruptions	inter	rupt	ion	s
1.	reporters	re	port	er	s
2.	transportation	trans	port	ation	
3.	supportively	sup (sub)	port	ive	ly
4.	deportees	de	port	ee	s
5.	importantly	im	port	ant	ly
6.	importers	im	port	er	s
7.	abruptly	ab	rupt	ly	
8.	disruptively	dis	rupt	ive	ly

Part B: *Words sometimes carry a positive or negative connotation, or feeling. Color the more positive words yellow, and the more negative words a different color. Leave neutral words blank.* Answers will vary. No key.

abrupt	important	corruption	supportive
disruptive	interruption	transport	corrupt
portable	rupture	abruptly	suicidal
claustrophobic	anachronism	pandemonium	zoophobia
pathogen	psychopath	telepath	telephone
reporters	aquarium	bio-terrorism	thermos

Part A: *Fill in the lines with words taken from the word bank. Look for clues in the sentence.*

inscription	scribe	subscription	transcription
manuscript	scribble	prescribe	scripts

Example: An _____inscription_____ has been inscribed on the tombstone.

1. The typist will transcribe a _____transcription_____ of the meeting notes.

2. Long ago, only a _____scribe_____ could read or write.

3. Dr. Phillips will _____prescribe_____ antibiotics for his patient.

4. Little children _____scribble_____ before they learn to write.

5. The author submitted a _____manuscript_____ to the publisher.

6. Michelle got a _____subscription_____ to that teen magazine for her birthday.

7. Have the actors and actresses memorized their _____scripts_____?

Part B: *For each word, list related words with different suffixes (some possible suffixes: -ion, -ive, -able, -ly, -ity, -or, -er).*

distract	contract	subtract	attract
distraction	contractual	subtraction	attraction
distractable	contraction	subtrahend	attractive
distractively	contractor	subtractive	attractively

Answers will vary.

The Latin root **cept** *(cep, capt, cap)*

Part A: *Deconstruct each word. Write each morpheme. Discuss how clearly these words convey the root meaning of 'to take or to seize.' Write* **Yes** *or* **Somewhat**. *For example, in football, an* **interception** *happens when we* **take** *or* **seize** *the ball, so we write* **Yes**.

	Word	Prefix	Root	Suffix	Suffix	Word conveys meaning of 'to take or to seize'
Example:	interceptions	inter	cept	ion	s	Yes
Example:	perceptively	per	cept	ive	ly	Somewhat (if you take my meaning!)
1.	recaptured	re	capt	ure	ed	Answers will vary, but encourage discussion and critical thinking.
2.	captivity		capt	ive	ity	
3.	deceptively	de	cept	ive	ly	

Part B: *Morphotextual Mastery: Read. Discuss the boldface words. Paraphrase.*

Imperceptibility

The Roman civilization began very small, about 600–700 years B.C. Rome expanded its territory, at first imperceptibly, bit by bit. The empire grew enormous, stretching from England to Africa. Finally, the great city of Rome "fell" (about 410 years after Christ). Why did the empire collapse? **Historians** agree that imperceptible but powerful changes took place over the **millennium**, leading to Rome's downfall.

What were these **imperceptible** changes? The most important change had to do with **responsibility**. At first, Romans personally took care of their land. They protected and improved their cities. These early Romans were **perceived** as diligent, responsible, and actively involved. They were tough and they cared passionately for home and hearth.

However, over the centuries, almost **imperceptibly**, a new attitude emerged. The rich Romans grew lazy and **self-indulgent**. They paid others to take over so they could relax and enjoy their fine mansions and leisurely lifestyles. Instead of fighting their own battles, they paid soldiers to protect their borders. They paid managers to control their farms. Instead of planting their own crops, they forced **captives** to do it. Romans became fat and **complacent**. However, they were not **indestructible**, not **invulnerable**, not **invincible**.

Gold cannot buy responsibility or **integrity**. The soldiers they purchased were mercenaries who only fought for money. Similarly, the farm managers only served themselves. They stole from the Roman landowners, **deceiving** them. In this way, gradually, Rome grew weak. Rome grew **vulnerable**. It was **inconceivable** at the time, but when hungry hordes of invaders attacked, Rome collapsed . . . and the Dark Ages began.

The Latin root **spect (spec, spectra)**

Select five vocabulary words from the prior pages, highlighting the roots and underlining any affixes. Beneath, write the meaning of the prefix and root, as shown in the example. Write the grammatical word class under the suffix. Look back in the book for help.

Answers will vary, based on word choice.

Example:	in	spect	ion		
	inside	to look	(noun)		
1.					
2.					
3.					
4.					
5.					

BONUS ACTIVITY   Multisensory, see page 229

Part A: *Write at least six words containing* **ject** *('to throw') and the affixes listed below.*

prefixes	de-	ob-	re-	pro-	in-
suffixes	-ion	-ure	-ive	-ile	-or

conjecture	dejection	rejection
projectile	etc. (answers will vary)	

Part B: *Highlight the correct word found in parentheses.*

1. Another word for teacher is (instructor, instructive).

2. A fallen tree in the road will (obstruction, obstruct) traffic.

3. To build the model airplane, he followed the (instructing, instructions) carefully.

4. Sometimes criticism can be helpful and even (constructive, destructive).

5. Strong winds nearly caused that (destruct, structure) to collapse.

6. Perjury, or lying under oath, is an (obstruction, obstruct) to justice.

The Latin root dict (dic)

Part A: *Join the morphemes together to form a complete word. Drop the final vowel before adding a suffix that begins with a vowel.*

	Morphemes				Whole word
Example:	dict	ate	or		dictator
1.	pre	dict	ion	s	predictions
2.	un	pre	dict	able	unpredictable
3.	contra	dict	ion	s	contradictions
4.	juris	dict	ion		jurisdiction
5.	bene	dict	ion		benediction
6.	in	dic	ate		indicate
7.	in	dic	ate	or	indicator
8.	val-e	dict	or	ian	valedictorian
9.	in	dic	ate	ive	indicative
10.	dict	ion	ary	es	dictionaries
11.	dict	ate	or	i-al	dictatorial
12.	pre	dict	able	ity	predictability

Part B: *Highlight all positively connoted words yellow.*   Answers will vary.

dictator	dictionary	unpredictable	malediction
benediction	dictate	contradict	diction
obstruction	dejected	constructive	instructive
destructive	respectable	captive	deception
scripture	subtract	corrupt	astronaut

The Latin root mit (mitt, mis, miss)

Part A: *Write at least eight words with the root **mit**, **mitt**, **mis**, **miss** ('to send') and the affixes listed below.*

prefixes	dis-	o-	re-	ad-	com-	trans-	sub-
suffixes	-ion	-ary	-ile	-al	-er	-ive	-s

dismiss	mission	admit
	etc. (answers will vary)	

Part B: *Highlight the correct word in parentheses.*

1. The malfunctioning furnace will not (omit, (emit)) heat.

2. The exhaust from cars sends toxic ((emissions), submissions) into the atmosphere.

3. She needed a new radio (translator, (transmitter)).

4. Send a facsimile (commission, (transmission)) to your loan officer.

5. It was critically important that they complete their (admission, (mission)) successfully.

6. During the war, both rockets and (missives, (missiles)) were fired.

7. ((Omission), Admission) to the concert will cost $24.00.

8. I will (remiss, (dismiss)) the students at three o'clock.

9. The captive would not (commit, (submit)) to his jailors.

The Latin roots **flex** (**flect**) *and* **cred**

Part A: *Choose a word from the word bank to match the definition. One word is a decoy; do not use it.*

deflect	flexible	flexibility	genuflect
reflector	flexor	reflect	(flex)

Example: to bend   <u>flex</u>

1. able to be bent   <u>flexible</u>

2. to bend back (often with light)   <u>reflect</u>

3. a device used to reflect light   <u>reflector</u>

4. to bend your knees in worship   <u>genuflect</u>

5. a muscle that bends a joint   <u>flexor</u>

6. the ability to bend easily   <u>flexibility</u>

Part B: *Write the root and the meaning of the root (not the meaning of the whole word).*

	Term	Root	Meaning
Example:	incredibility	cred	to believe
1.	subterranean	terra	earth, rocks
2.	transportation	port	to carry, to bear
3.	mortal	mort	death, to die
4.	accredit	cred	to believe
5.	aquarium	aqua	water
6.	tractor	tract	to pull
7.	disruptively	rupt	to break
8.	captivity	capt	to take, to seize
9.	rejection	ject	to throw
10.	predictions	dict	to say, tell, speak

Select five vocabulary words from the prior pages, highlighting the roots and underlining any affixes. Beneath, write the meaning of the prefix and root, as shown in the example. Write the grammatical word class under the suffix. Look back in the book for help.

Answers will vary.

Example:	dis-	pell	-ing		
	away	push	verb		
1.					
2.					
3.					
4.					
5.					

BONUS ACTIVITY   **Multisensory, see page 231**

Fill each leafy cluster with words that contain the root **press**. *Arrange words in related groups on the cluster, as shown in the example.* TIP: *Some words are given on the opposite page, but more words could be created by adding different affixes.*

(Answers may vary.)

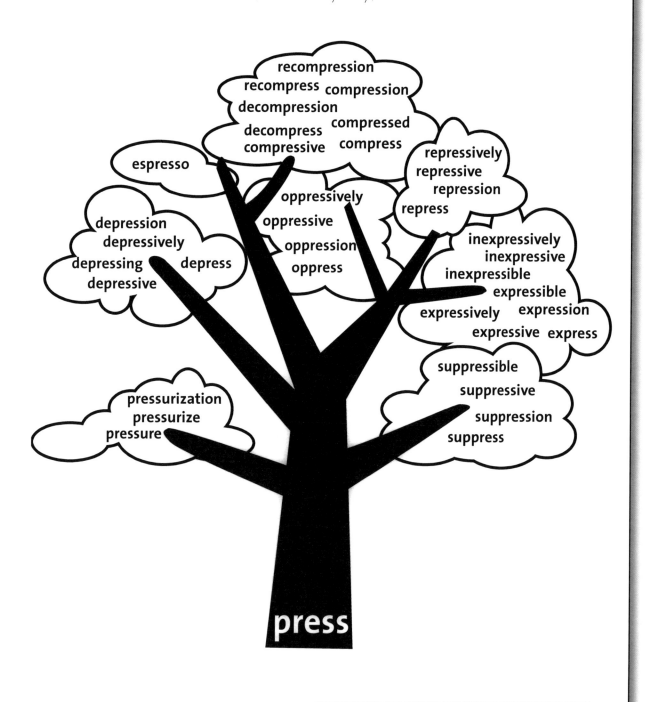

recompression
recompress compression
decompression
decompress compressed
compressive compress

repressively
repressive
repression
repress

espresso

oppressively
oppressive
oppression
oppress

depression
depressively
depressing depress
depressive

inexpressively
inexpressive
inexpressible
expressible
expressively expression
expressive express

suppressible
suppressive
suppression
suppress

pressurization
pressurize
pressure

press

BONUS ACTIVITY   **Multisensory, see page 233**

Assessment: Latin Roots

Write the root that matches the meaning. Roots are listed below (one of them is a decoy). The words in parentheses are clues; do not write them.

spect, spec (spectator)	script, scrib (scribble)	aqua (aquarium)
mis, mit (emit)	terra, terr (territory)	rupt (erupt)
dic, dict (dictionary)	struct (construction)	port (portable)
cept, cap (capture)	pel, pulse (propeller)	ject (reject)
mort (mortal)	tract (tractor)	(cred) (incredible)
flex, flect (reflection)	vert, vers (reverse)	"caveat emptor" (a motto)

Example: to believe — cred

1. to bend — flex, flect
2. to push, drive, move — pel, pulse
3. to build or devise or put together — struct
4. to send — mis, mit
5. take, seize, receive — cept, cap
6. to turn — vert, vers
7. watch, see, observe — spect, spec
8. to carry — port
9. to break — rupt
10. to throw — ject
11. to write — script, scrib
12. to say, to tell — dic, dict
13. to drag or pull — tract
14. water — aqua
15. death — mort
16. land, earth, soil — terra, terr

Final Assessment
Morphotextual Mastery: Suffixes, Prefixes, Roots

Discuss the title. Then read the passage silently. Highlight roots that you know. On the blank lines, write a suffix or prefix to complete the word. Finally, read the passage expressively.

The Wonders of Roman Engineering

If we begin with the legendary Romulus and Remus (~700 B.C.), the Roman civilization lasted more than a millennium. During this era, Rome changed technology forever. How? Romans were builders. They were excell_ent_ engineers, always dreaming up new ways to make their empire run more smoothly.

For example, to connect their vast territory they built a remark _able_ highway system. It was said, "All roads lead to Rome" (the capital city). A network of roads allowed the Romans to transport mail, import goods, and lead captives into captiv _ity_. On well-kept Roman roads, a chariot _eer_ could quickly transmit messages. Some Roman roads still exist today, _in_ credible as it sounds.

When Rome needed a more plenty _ful_ supply of fresh water, engineers designed aqueducts. To _con_ struct these aqueducts, they rerouted water from higher elevations. Roman aqueducts were capacious, bearing approximate _ly_ 14 million gallons of water into Rome daily, on average. Romans built arched bridges across the waterways. A few bridges are still in exist _ence_ today. Modern engineers marvel at such impress _ive_ workmanship.

When the emperor wanted a stadium for entertain_ment_, his brilliant engineer designed a masterpiece. In the coliseum, soldiers paraded, chariots raced, fabulous beasts performed. Gladiators fought in mort_al_ combat. At least 50,000 spectators crowded into the stadium. The Roman Coliseum still stands. The monument_al_ structure has endured, in spite of fires, earthquakes, erosion, and acts of vandal_ism_. It has been standing for near_ly_ 2,000 years! Is it _in_destructible? Not quite.

What was the secret to Roman engineering? How did these people man_age_ to accomplish such things? It's simple: Romans knew how to plan. They could organ_ize_ any task. It is true that Romans were marvel_ous_ engineers, but they did not invent or conceptualize every new design from scratch. Romans borrowed some ideas from the amazing Greeks who came before them. And the Greeks? Sailing the Mediterranean Sea, they adopted and internalized new ideas from every cult_ure_ in every port.

Today, we borrow from the Greeks and Romans—from other civilizations, too. Our world is built on the past. Our future is under construct_ion_ now.

Power Readers

Beginning Decodables for
Emergent Readers

Supercharged Readers

Decodable Chapter Books

with Jill Carroll

Daily Oral Vocabulary Exercises

A Program to Expand Academic
Language in Grades 4–12